VIOLATED
Perfection
Architecture and the Fragmentation
of the Modern

KEVIN MAGINNIS
wood, paint
No Title
1989

VIOLATED

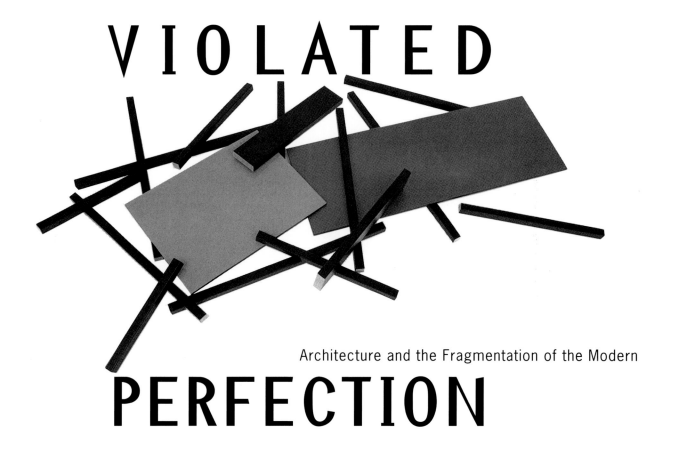

Architecture and the Fragmentation of the Modern

PERFECTION

AARON BETSKY
concept developed by Paul Florian, Stephen Wierzbowski and Aaron Betsky
with a violation by Paul Florian and Stephen Wierzbowski

RIZZOLI
NEW YORK

First published in the United States of America in 1990

Rizzoli International Publications, Inc.

300 Park Avenue South, New York, NY 10010

Library of Congress Cataloging-in-Publication Data

Betsky, Aaron.

Violated perfection: Fragmentation in modern architecture / Aaron Betsky.

p.   cm

ISBN 0-8478-1269-3. – ISBN 0-8478-1270-7 (pbk.)

1. Architecture, Modern--20th century.

2. Architects–Psychology.

I. Title

NA680.B497   1990   90-8399

724'.6–dc20   CIP

Designed by
LORRAINE WILD
assisted by
Barbara Glauber + Susan Parr
Composition in
Barry Sans, Bodoni Bold Italic,
and News Gothic.
Printed and bound in Japan.

front cover:
ATSUSHI KITAGAWARA
Rise Building
Tokyo, 1986
back cover:
AKS RUNO
The West Coast Gateway Project
1988

to my father

ACKNOWLEDGMENTS

This book was developed from an exhibition proposal of the same title assembled by Stephen Wierzbowski and Paul Florian at the University of Illinois at Chicago in 1986. In the course of a series of discussions in the spring of 1987, Paul, Stephen, and I developed the proposal for this book, and brought it to David Morton at Rizzoli International Publications. David believed in the project from the start, and his encouragement, advice and editorial assistance made this project possible. Paul and Stephen, without whom there would never have been a book, have continued to guide and inform the project. This is as much their book as it is mine. Frank Gehry offered his support and advice from the start, as did Philip Johnson. Joanne Heyler acted as the most intelligent and inventive research assistant I have ever known. My mother, Sarah Betsky Zweig, edited, and helped shape the initial draft and offered her invaluable insight, and Alda Trabucci of Rizzoli edited the final version. Lorraine Wild, with the assistance of Barbara Glauber and Susan Parr, helped bring order and visual clarity to the whole project.

During the course of writing this book, I had many valuable discussions. I am especially grateful to Tony Huertig, Bob Bruegman, Kurt Forster, Wes Jones, Tony Vidler, Thom Mayne, Lebbeus Woods and Jaime Rua for helping me to clarify my ideas. In addition, I must thank Celia McGee, Neil Denari, Charles Dilworth and Peter Haberkorn for their advice, support and good cheer.

Aaron Betsky

MORPHOSIS
ARCHITECTS
play sculpture
Cedars-Sinai Comprehensive
Cancer Clinic
Los Angeles, California, 1987

THE
TECHNO-SATYR

In the center of the Comprehensive Cancer Clinic, buried deep beneath the parking lot of the large Cedars-Sinai Medical Center in Los Angeles, stands a metal construction without any apparent function. Too strange, open, and kinetic to be a monument to the achievements of a deceased donor, too active to provide shelter or habitation, it appears alien – a giraffe-like metallic animal standing on slightly bent steel legs. Underneath the small hollow formed by its limbs, theater-like steps shelter disembodied television cameras and the unearthly glow of a fish tank. The construction is made of a scrim, stretched out like a memory of the lathe of which the wall was built, and rises to a plywood-paneled crown. Like the debris from another construction, a ladder remnant juts through it. The gridded plates on top of this beast tilt precariously forward, bending under the pressure of a small tree planted at its crown, reaching towards the liberating realm of a skylight at street level.

What is this construction? It lacks motivation. It does not seem to represent anything. It reverses our sense of proportion, gravity, and coherence. Why is this playful object buried three floors underground?

Is this "play sculpture" at the Comprehensive Cancer Center architecture? Yes. It condenses all elements comprising a critical architectural investigation. Its structure exhibits its own process of construction. Each rivet, bolt, and bend in the steel allows the viewer to understand the relationship between materials, elements outside of our bodily realm, and the human "artifacting," or construction necessary to order the object. This construction also condenses and foregrounds its own environment. Its legs mimic, in a deformed manner, the columns and pilasters at the base of the room in which it sits. Its body of sheets is a smaller scaled, collaged version of the layered walls of the enclosing room. Its openwork crown forces our attention to the top of the room, making us aware of another realm, illuminated by an unidentifiable natural source of light. In a most direct and tectonic manner, this piece of architecture articulates and makes visible a physical environment, thus allowing us to become conscious of our relationship with each other and our physical environment. Its legs, torso, and head stand in for our body, revealing skeletal and planar elements which are the essence of the building housing our body. It erects a narrative in which a mechanical stand-in for ourselves takes on properties from our environment before escaping into an unseen realm. The construction thus serves as a hybrid model for ourselves and that which contains us – a map of ourselves and our environment that suggests a way out of our body and the world of our creation.

The particular context of this play sculpture is marked by its extreme nature: it is a world inhabited by the terminally ill, people whose insides are transformed by an uncontrollable and alien transmutation. In the construction of this cancer clinic, its function, character, location, and philosophy have been represented architecturally. The clinic represents control, an entrance into a curing realm outside of the everyday in a technological quest. Such an experience is ambivalent. You descend into a tomb-like sequence of spaces comprised of gridded walls, floors, and ceilings – a prison in white where pointed metal light fixtures and bent steel balustrades protrude, uncomfortable reminders of the probing instruments hoping to heal. At the same time, many elements from classical architecture and the formal civic situation are at hand, introducing a preexisting and seemingly absolute order. As a passive subject to this control, you are passed through levels of initiations in low, labyrinthian corridors, losing all sense of a larger world and all sense of direction, finally

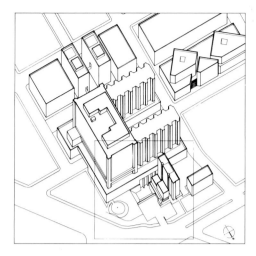

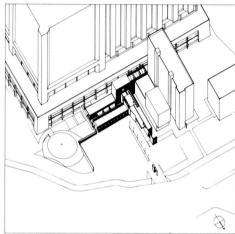

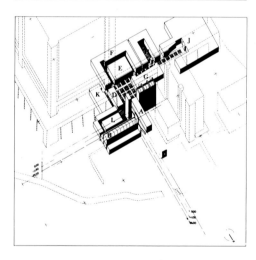

**MORPHOSIS
ARCHITECTS**
axonometrics
**Cedars-Sinai Comprehensive
Cancer Clinic**
Los Angeles, California, 1987

emerging into a realm of perfect peace and ethereal calm. Under the watchful gaze of nurses and television cameras, you are next subjected to machines that heal by way of destruction. You emerge, with part of you dead or dying, perhaps, or hairless, with a strange color. You have been transformed.

This environment represents the complete order and control that human culture claims to assert over humanity. Susan Sontag[1] uses cancer as a metaphor to describe how we must excise "the Other" from our body (politic). Max Horkheimer and Theodor Adorno describe all culture as an effort to deny the body and the self through domination and self-alienation. The root of all dialectics and thus of all suppression can be traced back to the moment when a human being defines itself as a body separate from the world, and thus as a subject to be operated upon.[2] For Jacques Derrida, a drug, or "pharmakon," rids the body of an unseen "other," and represents a metaphor for language itself.[3] The word allows us to bring forth what is hidden, to communicate, and ultimately establishes human culture. In the process it destroys the original whole of the singular body, replacing it with the subject of

healing or the subject of signification. The drug/language turns the body into an artifact, a mediated piece of culture that ceases to remember itself. Both sickness and its cure allow us to understand the overall relationship of modern society to the self. It provides a means for the elaborate construct of architecture, the most derived form of artifact, to retrace its roots.[4]

This is possible because at the point where a natural absolute – death – threatens the very existence of the self, man-made absolutes – science, control, and determined modes of behavior – show themselves. Remarkably, even at this point, architecture manages to hide systems of control that we submit to in our daily lives. The hospital surrounding the Comprehensive Cancer Clinic is made up of a series of banal blocks overpowering their context through their sheer scale. Carefully hidden by these boxes of absence are both the intricate and complex plan configurations and the myriad systems of plumbing, lighting, and air supply that are the inner reality of the center. This is traditional architecture: its forms have bottoms, middles, and tops. These are closed objects related to the human body through such scale devices as doors, windows, cornices, and signage (our current equivalent of expressive decoration). They say little, and only offer efficient and protective shelter. They affirm the reality of the unthinkable amount of man-made material that goes into them – the miles of pipes, steel, wood, carpeting, lights, plastic – and the reality of people encased in a shell made possible by the abstracted labor of many individuals. Especially when confronted with death, our society dissembles, hides, and affirms a bland status quo in which the related activities must be hidden behind blank walls, whether they be the interior partitions through which electrical cords mysteriously snake, the exterior curtain walls that make a health complex look like an office building, or the walls of conventions, declaring that expressive and chaotic representation are anathema to correct behavior and cultural artifacting.

The Comprehensive Cancer Clinic is not an affirming architecture; one might ask whether it is even a building. Other than its small sliver of an entrance lobby, nothing appears on the face of the city. It is not an "object," and thus does not confirm our notion that all activities must be housed in objects that control, and either hide or describe them. It has a non-hierarchical center or progression of rooms, so one cannot rationally understand and thus control the space by moving through it. The division between the publicly displayed and the privately hidden, which abrogates a complete and reciprocal control over the construction into which one enters in most buildings, has been broken down by a discontinuous arrangement of spaces with no obvious relationships.

The center does exhibit notions of control, although not literally. There is no false exhibitionism of ducts and wires. One cannot understand the building just by seeing or even touching its parts. Nor is there nostalgia for a rambling, anti-rational escape into a biomorphic land, nor an equally romantic crafting of "natural" materials. Such strategies of distraction and avoidance are replaced by a representation, a mapping and mirroring, of the condition of the modern, that is to say, of a world in which technology and its social derivatives completely control our world. The grids that make up the walls are layered and splayed to contain the overlapping systems of control: the joints that hammer the whole complex into shape are displayed, and each piece is a microcosm of the whole. In the disjunctive and fragmented composition of the clinic, the ordered rooms seem rhetorical, aware of their own position, like someone who starts shouting and suddenly realizes that everybody is listening. Then, at the center of all of this, is the claim for redemption.

At the base of the play sculpture, fish tanks remind us of another world, the world before culture. Television cameras film us as we move through the small theater of our world: monitors hanging from the sculpture force us to look at ourselves. The construction itself is both a larger version of our own body and a condensed image of technology, a small crane building itself. It suggests that we can look at ourselves and transform ourselves into something that is a vital part of this world, rather than its prisoner. Then we can rise up to a new ground plan, where the tree grows, liberated, to enter a new nature.

This is a romantic and liberating message. It is one fragment of an architectural investigation into the conditions of the world in which we live. If we can define our world as a modern one, and modernity as a consciousness of this world, which is characterized by continual technological change – a dynamic system of production and consumption that creates a profound instability in everything from social conditions to the physical environment – then that consciousness must continually wrestle with defining itself. It will always represent the conditions on which it reflects or that it knows, while attempting to create reactions or escapes. Architecture, along with accepted manners of behavior such as "legible" language, politics, and most other cultural constructs, acts as the artificial consciousness of the modern world, as that which attempts to present an aura of stability and continuity in order to perpetuate relative relationships of economic and social power. Modernity or modernism is not a "look" or historical period, but a definition of a consciousness of processes of modernization, of continual change and perfection in how things are made, how society operates. As such, modern architecture can only mirror or map our world.

Yet the design of the Comprehensive Cancer Clinic seems to reassemble the elements of a mirror that is deliberately cracked, a map that offers a way out. One might say that the play sculpture is satiric. It is a third kind of architecture, neither tragic and filled with *a priori* meaning, nor comic, vernacular, and part and parcel of our daily lives. The Comprehensive Cancer Clinic offers a romantic alternative, a monstrous hybrid form of criticism. It does so first by making visible the sheer power, complexity and oppressiveness of architecture as the physical realization of systems that are the armature of technology, but which are usually hidden behind the anonymity of architecture. It then proposes a violation, a breaking apart and questioning, of those systems. That violation is made possible by the search for perfection, the dream that there is something that is so much the perfect representation of the conditions of the modern world that it negates itself, negates us, negates the world. Each maker (architect) believes that he or she is engaged in an authentic act that is free from, and thus violates, all systems of control. By asserting that possibility, one builds. Yet in building, one violates any possible perfection, since what is constructed will always be of his world. What is important is the acceptance both of the drive for perfection and freedom, and the belief that such liberation must be achieved in the modern, as it is breaking apart. The activity of architecture can thus become a means to break down the abstract and ever-changing systems of technological control into formats that will allow us, collectively, to alter them and reassert the primacy of communal activity without a productive end.

The architectural activity of communal making rather than individual production is able to confront any built affirmation of the status quo. This effort to escape the dilemma of the individual struggle with the modern world, a willful struggle against the affirmation of architecture as the negation of a critical making, is the subject of this book. The process by which architecture became modern – a conscious representation of the processes of modernization – will first be discussed, followed by a proposal of critical and empowering strategies of resistance for engaging us with our manmade world. This focus on specific works and failed attempts, one hopes, will loosen our "mind-forged manacles." In the following text, Los Angeles provides a center for a discussion of predominantly American works. From amidst this most modern of metropoles, in a country which invented itself, the "project of the modern" will be examined and examples proposing its violation will be provided.

Los Angeles, 1990

HOLT, HINSHAW, PFAU, JONES
Primitive Huts Project
1985

1. Sontag, Susan. *Illlness as Metaphor.* New York: Farrar, Strauss, and Giroux, 1978.
2. Horkheimer, Max, and Theodor W. Adorno. *Dialectic of Enlightenment.* Transl. by Joan Cumming.New York: The Seabury Press, 1969. pp. 49ff.

3. Derrida, Jacques. "Plato's Pharmacy," *Dissemination.* Transl. by Barbara Johnson. Chicago: The University of Chicago Press, 1981 (1972), pp. 61-172.

4. Foucault, Michel. *Madness & Civilization. A History of Insanity in the Age of Reason.* Transl. by Richard Howard. New York: Vintage Books, 1973 (1961).

DANIEL H. BURNHAM,
RICHARD MORRIS HUNT
ET.AL.
Court of Honor seen from east
World's Columbian Exposition
Chicago, Illinois, 1893
Photo: Avery Architectural
and Fine Arts Library,
Columbia University, New York

THE PROJECT
OF
THE MODERN

What is the project of the modern? It is the exploration of the possibilities created by technology that give a guiding structure to its transformational potential. Since technology, if defined as a means to an end, is predicated on the transformation of the world by the conscious activities of man, this project is certainly an ancient one. Modernity, however, is the consciousness that man and nature have indeed become separate. Man now acts upon nature, with the potential of replacing nature with a new and complete world. Ironically, this process may ultimately achieve the destruction of man, since every aspect of his reality not subject to control, rationalization and change could be destroyed. This is Faust and Mephistopheles' bargain, realized in all revolutionary dreams of a new man. In the realm of the modern, it is a utopia which man continually recrafts with logic and rationalization out of the basic dialectic between production and consumption – one in which man and the world will eventually become synonymous with technology itself.

The project of the modern is the imaginative organization of the processes of modernization – very real processes such as changes in the ways things are made, but also more intangible changes such as those affecting social relations or how we create images of ourselves. Architecture is central to this process as a physical fact, an organizing force, and a metaphor. This text will focus on how the project of the modern has determined architectural form and practice in this century.

In the last one hundred years, despite nostalgic attempts to resurrect such tasks, architecture seems to have completely lost any connection with building as a mediator between man and nature, or as a ritualistic representation of human society, and has become instead a rationalized engine of change itself. Architecture is tending towards a situation in which it will no longer merely control or contain modernization, but will be modernization, or rather, its projection. The question then may be asked: if this identification is about to be achieved, has architecture not lost its autonomy and purpose? Is there such a thing as architecture anymore? Is there an alternative definition of architecture?

Central to a discussion of these questions is the realization that architecture has had the choice, at least since the late nineteenth century, of confronting this situation, or of avoiding it. This dilemma similarly exists in the social sphere. Although this choice was originally defined by the question of the ownership of the means of production, it is by now becoming clear that the central issue is one of empowerment:

who controls modernization itself,

that is to say,

who controls and defines the project of the modern? The role of architecture has been to contain, perpetuate in physical form, and thus conceal such control. Can architecture instead work towards the atomization of such control, thus helping to change the nature of modernization itself? To do so, it must first neither control, contain nor conceal, but represent the "beast" that is modernization in its fullest form. Ironically, it must first fulfill the project of the modern, and, in so doing, turn it into a visible artifact that can be then be critically altered by its users, inhabitants, and respondents.

There are thus two architectural models in the twentieth century: one that controls, contains, and conceals processes of modernization with false images of order, validated by the past and seen as existing outside of those processes, and one that plunges headlong into the project of the modern, seeking to construct and become "the monster." That monster takes the form both of the great metropolis, the stage of modernization, and of the machines that are its acting mechanisms and its hallmark images of repetition. In 1901, Frank Lloyd Wright confronted that city in a lecture at the Hull House in Chicago, entitled "The Arts and Crafts of the Machine":

Be gently lifted at nightfall to the top of a great down-town office building, and you may see how in the image of material man, at once his glory and menace, is this thing we call a city.

There beneath, grown up in night, is the monster leviathan, stretching acre upon acre into the far distance....Ten thousand acres of cellular tissue, layer upon layer, the city's flesh, outspreads enmeshed by intricate networks of veins and arteries, radiating into the gloom, and there with a muffled, persistent roar, pulses and circulates as the blood in your veins, the ceaseless beat of the activity to whose necessities it all conforms....

Its nerve ganglia – the peerless Corliss tandems whirling their hundred ton fly-wheels, fed by gigantic rows of water tube boilers burning oil...the incessant clicking, dropping, waiting-lifting, waiting, shifting of the governor gear controlling these modern Goliaths....

And the texture of the tissue of this great thing, this Forerunner of Democracy, the Machine, has been deposited particle by particle, in blind obedience to organic law, the law to which the great solar universe is but an obedient machine. This is the thing into which the forces of Art are to breathe the thrill of ideality! A SOUL![1]

In this fearful and fearsome vision, Wright embraces modernization in all its might. Just as Karl Marx had called up the power of the machine in all of its natural logic[2] and had triumphantly proclaimed that "All that is solid melts into air...";[3] so Wright takes on the aggressive, anti-human aspects of the machine, its space- and time-defying, rationalizing and abstracting potential, as the harbinger of not so much a new world, as of a new organism, a city, body and machine all at the same time, producing a new text for itself.

Wright's thesis is that mechanized mass production is taking over all aspects of our existence, from the production of language to the creation of what were formerly considered art objects. Rather than merely lamenting or fighting this process, Wright proposes that architects appropriate the development. Craft and mechanical production were, in his opinion at the time, not opposites. Rather, the latter was the natural outgrowth of the former. The designer could become the equivalent of the modern manager, organizing the efforts of craftsmen working together in cooperatives in order to create objects of everyday use that would be more "poetical": "The new will weave for the necessities of mankind…a robe of ideality more poetical, with a rational freedom made possible by the machine."[4] Wright here embraces the idea of remaking the world, of creating a man-made world through technology, as both a frightening fact and an appeal to utopia. The difference is the role of design, of the consciousness of this fact, in the process. As such, Wright offered an updated version of the beliefs of John Ruskin, William Morris and their followers, according to whom it was in the actual involvement in the making of objects of everyday use, and in the designing of these objects in such a way that they represented formalized versions of an otherwise incomprehensible universe, that the model and building blocks of a new society could be created.[5]

Wright sought to reintroduce the notions of this arts and crafts community by embracing machine production and, more importantly, its consequences. Architecture was to be an act of carving out and revealing a man-made version of nature. This reductive activity was to be part of an overall drive toward abstraction and minimalization which mimicked the logic of the machine and of a rationalized (that is, text-based) society.[6] The production of these objects could be, as noted above, similarly rationalized into efficient groups of specialized workers under the guidance of an architect/manager.[7] And just as the process and object of production had become abstract, defying the closed nature of the object or its making, so the architecture which defines, represents, and houses these activities must become more open and abstract – a simple skeleton of pure structure.[8]

What Wright proposed was the active destruction of all that stood between the reality of the world and our ability to work on that world. He wanted to remake our world by crafting in a cooperative, communal way.[9] In the end, there would be no more architecture or art to look at, only the traces of the carving and a structure for human activity. What would be visible would be the mechanized city, which we would then recognize as ourselves and our extension, the machine. The final image is that of a city, a machine and man as one. Architecture then would become the meta-machine, the machine that is about (our own) mechanization.

In positing this vision, Frank Lloyd Wright was reacting against the dominance of American classicism and its willful ignorance of the reality of modernization. He opposed his man/machine/building to architecture as a separate object between man and nature, a tool for using nature. Wright opposed the notion of architecture as a cultural ordering device. Such an architecture was a way of understanding the world, controlled by the architect and the client. It presented the myth that a unified control over processes of modernization was possible. That is what Henry Adams had thought when he visited the 1893 World's Columbian Exposition. Standing in its white classical world, he exclaimed:

Chicago asked in 1893 for the first time the question whether the American people knew where they were driving. Adams answered, for one, that he did not know, but would try to find out. On reflecting sufficiently deeply, under the shadow of Richard Hunt's architecture, he decided that the American people probably knew no more than

HENRY VAN BRUNT
Electricity Building
World's Columbian Exposition
Chicago, Illinois, 1893
Photo: The Art Institute of Chicago

he did; but that they might still be driving or drifting unconsciously to some point in thought, as their solar system was said to be drifting towards some point in space; and that, possibly, if relations enough could be observed, this point might be fixed. Chicago was the first expression of American thought as unity; one must start there.[10]

What Adams saw was a unified image of American culture in a condition of modernization using the medium of architecture. The World's Columbian Exposition was not meant to mirror or represent American society at large, but to express one version of it from the fixed perspective of those in control. As Alan Trachtenberg has so admirably described in his essay "White City,"[11] the exhibition was meant literally to build the notion of the manifest destiny of American industrial society.[12]

The fair's central portion was covered with a thin veneer of culture built up of classical elements with a papier-mâché-like material called *staff*. Entered through an overwhelming portico that dwarfed the human figure and introduced one into another realm, the Court of Honor pointed out to the undefined, and as yet unconquered, horizon of Lake Michigan, towards which Columbia was being driven

by an efficient set of allegorical oarsmen.[13] The buildings around this court were individual objects isolated by waterways. They were connected only by their common cloth of white paint and Beaux-Arts ornament. Each object contained, literally and figuratively, one aspect of the great engine of modernization which converted, what at that time seemed like boundless resources, into consumable artifacts: agriculture, industry, transportation, machinery, mines and electricity.

Henry Van Brunt's Electricity Building may stand in for all of these temples to progress. A perimeter colonnade of Corinthian columns established a precinct, which one could then enter either through an apsidal space defined by a giant archway, or through a colonnade whose double towers and pedimented central section offered an ecclesiastical alternative to the imperial entrance. A world thus described by all the weight of a correct, if inventively combined, inventory of architectural shapes (and thus by two thousand years of allusions to power) then suddenly opened up into another realm. Rather than containing a central and a subsidiary cross axis leading to first major and then secondary spaces, the interior was almost completely taken up by two crossing halls for the display of machinery and electrical gadgets. Here the comfort of classicism gave way to an open network of metal members rising up in delicate arches that spanned the width of the halls. The roof itself seemed to float above a band of clerestory lights. Placed inside of this ethereal, non-directional and thoroughly modern space were the machines: enigmatic and strangely formed objects sometimes bursting under a cover of applied decoration.[14]

The Electricity Building contained the new world, a world without hierarchy or clear signification, made

ferris wheel, midway
World's Columbian Exposition
Chicago, Illinois, 1893
Photo: The Art Institute of Chicago

of new materials at a new scale. But it contained within it an architecture that reasserted control over this world: a control of scale, familiar forms, rhythms and hierarchies, but also a control of order, legibility and singularity. The new world of freedom and untold possibilities had to be controlled by an agreed upon civil authority. This cultural control was Adams' "virgin," culture married to progressive and rational politics, education, and the other values by which the ruling class of late nineteenth- and early twentieth-century America justified itself and its control.[15]

What could not be controlled was exiled: exiled from architecture, culture, and the center of the fair. Beyond the peristyle was that which was to be operated upon, the new and chaotic nature to be conquered and subdued by technology, and covered with culture: the city of Chicago into which the long umbilical cord of the Midway reached with its hodgepodge of non-architectural shacks for entertainment and unabashed consumption of fantasy. The Midway was the place of complete freedom, where the masses could cavort. Ironically, it was also the place of complete clarityl. At the center of the Midway one could ride the first Ferris Wheel and rise up over the whole construct of the fair to put it into context. At the base of this "wheel of escape," Eadweard Muybridge exhibited his time-

HENRY VAN BRUNT
interior, Electricity Building
World's Columbian Exposition
Chicago, Illinois, 1893
Photo: Avery Architectural
and Fine Arts Library,
Columbia University, New York

lapse photography, a prototype of the cinema that brought objects and scenes of far-away places and times to all, not just the privileged few. These inventions were unfettered by the bounds of decency and architecture. This was the place of chaos, non-linearity, technology, and of endless, diffused, and instantaneous possibilities. This was Wright's metropolis, but to the makers of the fair it was neither culture nor architecture.

The fair thus formalized a false unity of American thought, a veneer of purpose and control that found its expression and representation in American classicism,[16] commissioned by the few who controlled, and designed by the even smaller new group of male, white professionals known as architects.[17] Adams' dynamo, the virile reality of American modernization, and Wright's vision of how to use that dynamo, were either contained or exiled from the mainstream of the definition of our society. The exhibition of and education for a set of values that would justify that central cultural control became the main overt task of the self-perpetuating elite as it extended its control over reality ever further.

Ever since 1893, when the World's Columbian Exposition only formalized processes well underway, most American architecture, as well as architecture almost everywhere in the world, has operated according to this principle of the repression and exile of modernity.[18] One can, in fact, reduce most public architecture in this century, regardless of its style, to the few characteristics exhibited and formalized at that fair.

They are all self-contained objects that mask more or less complicated activities in order to give them a unified signification. They are controlled by a commissioner, and mediated through the generalizing activity of an architect (male, white) seeking to subsume this particular expression under a consensus culture. These objects are placed within the city grid, accepting its abstract and rational order. They are plugged into a civic structure, which reaches from the public language of the architectural denotation to the invisible structure of electricity and sewage systems. They are designed as part of a bureaucratic process, and their functional plan arrangements reflect this process: the rationalization of activities into separate realms, organized around, and hidden by an empty realm of symbolic lobbies, hallways, stairways and courts.

These are intricate machines concerned with the mediation of technology by culture. This is "American thought as unity," and in 1908 Daniel Burnham dreamed of extending this vision to cover literally the whole city. This dream was partially realized in Chicago, San Francisco, Cleveland and Washington, to name only the cities in which Burnham was involved, and picked up again by those urban planners seeking to clear the chaos of the slums – deplorable because of their horrible conditions and also because they still showed some signs of communal activity – with the revealing clarity of empty lots of gridded buildings in the downtowns of the 1950s and 1960s.

Frank Lloyd Wright's resistance to this development remained isolated. Given his later career, his Hull House speech seems like an isolated illumination in a life dedicated to monument making.

GERRIT RIETVELD
Schröeder House
Utrecht, The Netherlands, 1925
Photo: Centraal Museum, Utrecht

In this century America has seemed to be a nation at the forefront of modernization; but it was in Europe, where architects were fascinated by the heroic reality of American modernization, that a tradition born in the arts and crafts movement exploded the notion of architecture from the inside out. European architects started with an overwhelming context which actively obstructed the new and the chaotic both with idiosyncratic and accretional forms, and with grand orders alluding to past grandeur. They turned to the arts and crafts tradition as a means of liberating the machine from the oppression of a historically determined status quo and, with that mechanical man-made beast, themselves. The two great laboratories for the creation of modern design, the Staatliche Bauhaus in Germany, and the Vkhutemas in Russia, were outgrowths of the same kind of romantic arts and crafts movements that had so inspired Frank Lloyd Wright.

However, the paradigm for the active deconstruction of the established world may be found in the Schröeder House, designed in Utrecht in 1924 by Gerrit Rietveld. Rietveld was trained as a furniture maker and came from a family dedicated to that

profession – a background that stands in marked contrast to the academic and pseudo-scientific character of the architectural profession, especially in Germany.[19] He thus came to architecture from the outside, and felt no need to create monumental "condensations" of the spirit of the time, as did such luminaries of Dutch modernism as H.J.P. Berlage or J.J.P. Oud.[20] Instead, he started from the inside out, taking apart simple objects of

GERRIT RIETVELD
interior, second floor
Schröeder House
Utrecht, The Netherlands, 1925
Photo: Centraal Museum, Utrecht

structural components or compositional elements. When he received the commission for the Schröder house, he was faced with a truly avant garde situation: the house was to be situated at the end of a long row of petit bourgeois row houses at the very edge of the city, where the closed-in urban environment with its dark red brick walls gave way to the horizontal and expansive order of the gridded fields. The house takes the walls of the rowhouses and, starting with the massive party walls, pulls them apart, rotates them and floats them off of the concrete slabs that were hidden in the older constructions. The walls were then painted in primary colors, abstract and weightless emblems of nothingness, as if nothing needed to be signified about living in a house, beyond the fact that physical resources are assembled around a core. This central element, painted a neutral gray, protruded

from the top of the house. It contained the major vertical circulation, which was lit by a gridded skylight-box and wrapped around the sewage pipes and electrical conduits.

The core and the fragmented walls were the only fixed elements in the house. On the ground floor, space was partitioned for such activities as sleeping and studying, but on the second floor, the *piano nobile*, where the real activity of living took place, there were nothing but movable partitions that could accommodate a large variety of spatial configurations. The furniture was reduced to a series of functional and unexpressive planes or combinations of structural members (such as was the case in the famous red-yellow-blue chair of 1919), and the radiators and windows were made of uncovered industrial materials. The house had a no-nonsense air, using mass-produced materials in such a logical manner that one can understand how they were manufactured and how they extend the human body into space. When the windows were all open, and the walls were all pulled back, the second floor of the Schröeder house truly became the liberated new space made possible by technology and inhabited by beings "extending themselves into mechanization." The space flowed out of the windows into the adjacent fields, a cultured and artifacted "paradise regained."[21] This house remains a paradigmatic representation of the project of the modern.

The ideological foundation for such designed deconstructions was supplied by painters such as Theo van Doesburg and Piet Mondrian as well as architects. These founders of the magazine *De Stijl*, which gave its name to the movement, were convinced that art (and architecture) – as the creation of isolated objects commenting on, but outside of everyday life – was becoming increasingly

THEO VAN DOESBURG
(in collaboration with Cornelis van Eesteren)
Color Construction: Project for a Private House
1922
Collection The Museum of Modern Art, New York

obsolete: "'Art' (in the traditional sense) is progressively dissolving.... Simultaneously, outward life is becoming fuller and many-sided, thanks to rapid transportation, sports, mechanical production and reproduction."[22] The role of the artist/architect was to create "architecture-as-environment" out of the merger of architecture, sculpture, painting and decorative arts.[23] The role of this art was to bring out the abstract, spiritual character of life, which until now had remained hidden by the objects of the material world, by tradition, and by ignorance.

In this justification lies the weaknesses of the neo-plasticist theories, and of most European theoreticians building a new world between the two World Wars. Unable to imagine a reworking of the visible world in such a way that each human being would be able to place him or herself confidently in that world, they could only envision its dissolution. They turned away from "if-not-this-then-what" towards a quasi-religious quest for pure abstraction and transparency. In the process, they became disconnected from the social activism that had fueled, and would continue to fuel, the architectural activity of many of the more radical designers. The research into radical alternatives for the recreation of closed forms, disconnected from the realities of rapidly developing systems of production, became associated with the creation of isolated art objects.[24] In contrast, the reductivism of Hannes Meyer and J.J.P. Oud became associated with the streamlining of methods of production and architectural forms so that they might serve the needs of larger groups of people. Thus Oud might create a row of housing and paint it white and round its corners, as he did in 1925 in Rotterdam, but the project still presupposed that each family lived exactly the same lives within isolated and therefore tradition-reinforcing spaces (separate bedrooms, kitchens and living rooms). Hannes Meyer might

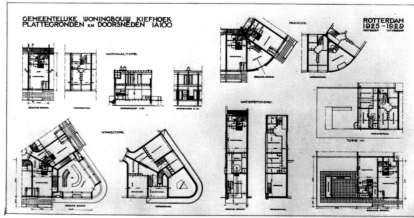

propose a League of Nations building that looked radically different from the symmetrical and closed forms of Beaux-Arts monuments, but it remained a series of blocks, composed *a priori* to meet an abstract set of planological and symbolic relationships.[25] Social activism thus implied merely an adaptation of new forms to existing social conditions. Mondrian remained within the realm of painting, that is to say, in the seamless representation of a new world of abstraction and liberation, but never carried through on its constitution,[26] while his executor manquée, Rietveld, toned down his revolutionary deformalization to meet the needs for mass housing.[27] As has been pointed out often,[28] the unfortunate result of the early modernists' effort to abstract, reduce and bring out the technological nature of an industrialized society was the creation of forms serving those in control of that society with increased efficiency, and subjecting more lives, including those of the working class who had ironically maintained their independent and idiosyncratic self-definitions in repression and exploitation,[29] to the harsh light of oppressive and alienated control.[30]

An alternative stance more fully responsive to artistic engagement than either those that created new forms in isolation or those that merely streamlined reality, was developed by those interested in process and technique. This expression can be traced from the Bergsonian futurists to the Bauhaus, the Dada movement, Russian constructivism, and suprematism. The Futurist Manifesto, that supreme call to modernization, recalls the fervor of Frank Lloyd Wright in its passionate embrace of the modern city:

We will sing the great masses agitated by work, pleasure, or revolt; we will sing the multicolored and polyphonic surf of revolutions in modern capitals; the nocturnal vibration of arsenals and docks beneath their glaring electric moons; greedy stations devouring smoking serpents; factories hanging from the clouds by threads of smoke....[31]

Their methodology, however, was radically different, and seemed to them a logical continuation of the very processes of modernization that did not need representation, because they represented themselves:

It is a question of...fulfilling to the limit every demand of our way of life and our spirit, of rejecting everything grotesque, cumbrous, and alien to us (tradition, style, aesthetic, proportion), establishing new forms, new lines, *a new harmony of profiles and volumes*, an architecture whose *raison d'être* lies solely in the special conditions of modern life, whose aesthetic values are in perfect harmony with our sensibility. This architecture cannot be subject to any law of historical continuity.... It must be as new as our frame of mind is new.[32]

To accomplish this end, Sant'Elia and Marinetti go on to say, the notion of architecture as the creation of monuments, of isolated objects, must be rejected in favor of a rethinking of the whole man-made environment.[33] In this, the futurists shared the views of the neo-plasticists. But they were burdened by its escapist spiritualism. By combining this kind of active deconstructive program with the belief that the very materials and forms of the industrialized landscape had already accomplished their goal, and only needed to be composed or "infused with spirit,"[34] the futurists avoided the problems of a self-consciously constructive and reductive avant-garde. Yet beyond any naive belief in the cooperative resistance of the American and English arts and crafts movements, they faced another dilemma. The creation of a futurist object immediately reversed the process of unveiling or unleashing the dynamic of modernization, and allowed it to be captured in forms that could be both consumed and understood by a bourgeois audience. The revolution ended as soon as the battle was covered up, and became a commemorative, although aggressive and unconventional, grouping.

Marinetti's death dream, the logical outcome of his position,[35] led to his embrace of the dark forces of fascism. Sant'Elia died in World War I. To the

Dadaists who disavowed the finished object, the problem was merely dissolved. Performance, both as theatrical production and as action, was art, and remains so to Dadaists of this day.[36]

The anarchistic strain in avant-garde art and architecture, and its connection to the political movement, is fully intentional. Its actions are proposed as the active pulling apart of the false coherence that culture and politics throw over the project of the modern through techniques such as juxtaposition, decontextualization, fragmentation, and changes in scale, material or proportion.

KURT SCHWITTERS
Merzbau (Reconstruction)
Hannover, Germany, 1920-1935
Photo: Sprengel Museum, Hannover

These techniques have analogies in textual manipulations,[37] but their importance lies in their ability to take the very stuff out of which our world is made and, without adding anything to it, or presupposing an absolute order, manipulating it to recreate an alternative and miniaturized order, senseless as a static and communicable sign. This work of bricolage is directly connected to the art-making of non-Western cultures, and provides an "artificial" antidote to the production of art in conditions of mechanization, although the vitality of this work and the adaptability of the bricolage tradition to technologically determined media seem to refute criticism of the hypocrisy of such activities.[38] It can be argued that the ability to map one's world by creating a microcosm composed of known elements, i.e. objects of everyday use, and the transformation of that map into something that is both anthropomorphic and an extension of the body into an artifact capable of engaging and altering the environment, is the fundamental activity of art-making, and all else is a derivative of this art.[39]

Yet Dada, surrealism and other conceptual movements never involved themselves with such an integrated and thorough activity, stopping instead at the collecting of material (Schwitters) or the recreation of totems for industrial society (Duchamp). Duchamp's *Large Glass, (The Bride Stripped Bare by Her Bachelors, Even,* 1915-1923) is, of course,

the most complete production of this movement, and perhaps one of the most complicated architectural investigations of the twentieth century. Both a mirror of the self and a window into another world, it tends to disappear as an object, leaving only the traces of its own making. Duchamp thus created a historical and spatial map of industrial society in soot, in the shadows of machines, and in systems of measurement and therefore judgment, which are incomprehensible to all but the "initiated" and empowered. This machine for self-representation describes our society, and its use of sex and frustrated desire to stand in for more agonizing dilemmas reduces, as Duchamp well understood, man to a machine.[40]

However powerful such works may be, they remained isolated and, in the end, defeated by the architecture in which they were inevitably placed. Only when those walls were blown apart could an art emerge that would actively engage modern culture. Such was the case, to a certain extent, with the original performances of Brecht's plays,[41] and even more so in the work of Russian revolutionary artists.

Russian artists and architects after 1917 imagined they were literally building a new world, even if precious few of their projects were ever constructed. While artists such as Kandinsky espoused mysticism, and the significant rationalist school insisted on unexpressive functionalism, the ever-evolving group of suprematist/constructivist artists argued for, and created, an art that reinvented function.[42] Malevich, the godfather of the movement, started with the same reductivist and abstractionist urge as Mondrian, reducing the world he reproduced to pure white on white.[43] However, he and his followers then began to build, creating whole fantastical cities of planes, lines and volumes – a new world of pure elements.[44] That pure world was, then, via tortuous debates over the "facture" or physicality of the artwork,[45] translated into building materials of a "real" new society, constructed roughly, in fragments, or in rhetorical flourishes, by Melnikov, Leonidov, Tatlin and others. Leonidov's student design for the Lenin Institute, an openwork globe and a cantilevered plane held rigid by thin and intersecting lines, was made more massive and enigmatic in his project for the Narkomtiazhprom or Commissariat of Heavy Industry on Red Square of 1934.[46] Inspired by the skyscrapers of New York,[47] Leonidov created a gridded tower that was seemingly always under construction, served by a cone tapered at top and bottom, a shape that could not be understood as having a specific function or scale. These buildings were left as fragments of a larger complex, marooned on a stepped platform, so that the pedestal (hollow and habitable – it contained a meeting hall) to the unified monument had no unified object to support, except for the functional innards of what might have been enclosed in a more massive and horizontal shape.[48] The Narkomtiazhprom's construction represents its own making. Its forms, enigmatic in scale, texture, and placement avoid preconceptions about what could be built. Its fragmentary nature refuses a rigid monumentality, reaching instead towards an untold time.

Leonidov and his fellow practitioners described a possible constructivist architecture: one representing itself as something made, a bricolage of industrial materials, an enigmatic and therefore magical object able to map unseen realms, an anthropomorphic machine whose fragmentary nature challenges the city's status quo. Romantically expressive, and aggressively new, this architecture was never built. Instead, Leonidov and others retreated into pastoral escapism, turning first to set design – the staging of a new world when the new world refused to stage itself – and then focusing on photography.[49]

Rodchenko's photography proved fruitful for architectural investigation, even if repressed for the remainder of the century. In the darkroom, any reality could be altered and recreated. Photography lends itself well to both bricolage and fragmentation – for an active pulling apart of and tinkering with reality is a given. Man Ray realized this potential,[50] as did Moholy-Nagy[51] and some of the more avant-garde filmmakers. More importantly, mainstream films, followed by television, actively set about reforming reality. As Benjamin pointed out near the beginning of this development, film has the power to effect the merger between man and machine, and to place the viewer/camera in a frag-mented, collaged world in which miracles of technological development have ended the necessities for stable spaces and their enclosures:

By close-ups of the thing around us, by focusing on hidden details of familiar objects, by exploring commonplace milieus under the ingenious guidance of the camera, the film, on the one hand, extends our comprehension of the necessities which rule our lives; on the other hand, it manages to assure us of an immense and unexpected field of action. Our taverns and our metropolitan streets, our offices and furnished rooms, our railroad stations and our factories appeared to have us locked up hopelessly. Then came the film and burst this prison-world asunder by the dynamite of the tenth of a second, so that now, in the midst of its far-flung ruins and debris, we calmly and adventurously go traveling. With the close-up, space expands; with slow motion, movement is extended. The enlargement of a snapshot does not simply render more precise what in any case was visible, though unclear: it reveals entirely new structural formations of the subject.[52]

Film, in other words, has done away with the need for architecture.

Indeed, the progress of technology and of mass media have made architecture increasingly irrelevant. Mondrian, Marinetti and Malevich's dream of the dissolution of architecture actually occurred as the result of a logical technological development. In the end, according to Jean Baudrillard, this development has created a world of "simulations." Space is no longer significant or even extensive, but made up of isolated cells of information; and reality is not representable, since representation, that merger between man and camera, has taken over: "[We live at the] end of the old illusion of relief, perspective and depth (spatial and psychological) bound to the perception of the object:[53] it is the entire optic, the view become operational on the surface of things, it is the look become molecular code of the object." In more conventional Marxist terms, one might say that a superstructure and consciousness, as defined by the ruling class, have infiltrated scenes of production and consumption to the point of masking over all signs of activity – of making, using, and living-in-the-world.

It is not just film and mass media that have made architecture irrelevant, however.

In economic terms, as Manfredo Tafuri has pointed out, architecture is losing its relevance as a profession. From a client's perspective, the sole aim of architecture is to further the efficiency of industrial processes and their derivatives. For this architecture is no longer necessary; space planning, engineering and codification will do. Subsequently the whole profession is run by these considerations. The traditional role of architecture as an integrated and condensed representation of society, or a single human being, has similarly been taken over by mass media.

What we are increasingly left with is an anti-monumental architecture, an architecture that diffuses into space planning, flexible arrangements (which can thus not be easily composed), and facades that reflect this central instability. When Daniel Burnham proposed his Plan for Chicago in 1908, the bulk of the plan was made up of proposals for traffic patterns, sewage systems, and other infrastructural concerns. Architecture, as noted above, would vanish into faceless blocks of identical heights whose forms were wholly determined by the shape of the roads.[54] While much of the plan was implemented over the next fifty years, the one piece of monumental architecture proposed for the city, a domed Civic Center (similar to Richard Morris Hunt's Administration Building at the Columbian Exposition), was supplanted by a freeway interchange – a fitting substitution, since the highly engineered elements of our infrastructure, whether they be dams to create electricity and bring water to the city, power plants, or roads, have replaced our urban monuments. Baron Haussman carved through Paris to focus on the Arc de Triomphe or on the Opera; Robert Moses just hacked, leaving houses huddled under the scaleless, non-hierarchical gestures of the highways.

After the New Deal and a last attempt at making civic monuments, architects have retreated from their task of defining the civic realm, responding instead to function by designing buildings as insignificant blank boxes, and letting public space escape out in between the offset buildings. The same is true in the residential sphere, where architects mass produce houses, one kind for the rich and another kind for the poor, in a landscape that is neither ordered nor natural, but chaotic and elusive.

It is architects who "push" architecture's disappearance into mass production and engineering that manage to recreate an architecture out of the representation of its own absence. The unrealizable architecture of utopia is the last refuge of the representational and significant composition of physical resources. Such was the case in Neutra's Rush City Reformed, a city of office blocks replicating the furrows of plowed fields, thus recalling an analogy between the cultivation of nature and the cultivation of man as a machined activity.[55] One can also point to Wright's Usonia, the prototype for the perfect suburb. Here there is no center – only the unrealized forms of living, working or schooling, distributed throughout the landscape without a single stable form or sense of scale.[56] Such a landscape is incomprehensible; there no single object is itself; everything is a component of the community's larger machine – a machine that remains hidden, for its true body is its hidden electrical lines and

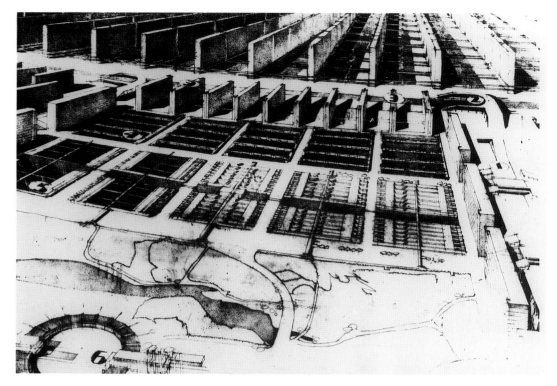

sewage systems, connecting roads, and an agreement to cooperate, maintaining the productivity of the greater whole. Architecture realizes itself in its own death.

Both American and European post-World War II modernism believed that only by embracing the destruction of the city, encouraging and justifying the abolishment of signification, and composing the break-up of stable forms could it save itself. It held onto a need to represent this very process of disappearance, leaving first articulated grids, then only the memory of grids in reflective glass panels, and then abstract and enigmatic tombs for these boxes of absence. Others, most notably Louis Kahn, constructed elegiac ruins, letting out heroic wails at the funeral of architecture. In the end, such gestures were irrelevant, which only added to the dark, mystical allure of the Howard Rourkian architect, struggling to keep alive the flame of some abstract spirit within the absence of architecture.

Over the last twenty-five years, numerous solutions to this problem have been proposed, countered by Tafuri's dictum that "No 'salvation' is any longer to be found within [modern architecture]: neither wandering restlessly in labyrinths of images so multivalent they end in muteness, nor enclosed in the stubborn silence of geometry content with its own perfection."[57] Neither the image-laden pastiches of the post-modernists, nor the self-consciously monumental reductions of the modernists can avoid the fact that their devices produce unnecessary artifacts and meaningless pieces of escapism, with one important exception: they sell the buildings.

And that is how modern architecture must be understood, despite a century of experimentation, or maybe (tragically) because of such experimentation. It neither justifies the whole process of modernization through representation, nor resists such processes, but rather is an activity promoting consumption. Space planners and engineers usurped the last foothold architects had in production, and thus architecture is no longer the bridge between those two sides of the cycle. Its facades merely present a public face to efficient production. Its detailing and compositional acumen "humanize," that is to say, present a false sense of individual scale and meaning to the activities housed. Its stylistic manipulations resurrect another world, removed in time and place from that of our modernized one. It creates a theatrical scene in which we can play roles more attractive than those to which we have been assigned. Architecture, in other words, sells our world to us. Architecture is an extension of advertising, but then every aspect of culture as industry has, in the end, no other function except to sell, whether specific products or their generalized context, "a way of life," a "lifestyle."

What remains is an architecture dedicated to realizing modernization through avoidance. Architecture now consists of the following. First, there are efficiently arranged places of everyday life. These spaces are given a place, but are generally not designed by architects. In the home, they are assembled out of mass produced elements into stereotypical arrangements which often impose patterns of behavior on the private lives of the inhabitants: breakfast rooms, master and other bedrooms, family rooms. They become training grounds for lifestyles, rather than part of a critical participation in the wider world. Work environments are arranged for the most efficient production possible, whether of goods or of services. Human beings are fit into machines, from office furniture assemblies to assembly robots. These machines/furnishings extend the body, enabling it to complete a task by turning the self into an extension of that task. Public spaces here either advertise for a company (lobbies), or offer efficient relaxation and nourishment for employees. Places for shopping are interiorized streets denying their physicality as much as possible with streamlined corners, hidden lighting, confounding axes, and walls dematerialized into individual display cases. The whole is completely cut off from any context.

All of this leads to more efficient consumption: architecture as a barrier is removed. In fact, the whole legal system is now bent on the negation of traditional architectural elements: smooth ramps, which elide the differences in groundplanes so important to defining the traditional architectural object, replace the striation of stairs. The traditional coherence of the object is also eroding, its multiple uses are becoming so complex that it is increasingly impossible even to define a single front door. Or, for instance, the car demands a complicated entrance sequence whose jumps in scale and form of movement are almost impossible to legislate in any coherent design. Finally, any imagery of authority, or dignity, is eroded by our inability to agree on any one center of power, or any coherent expression of civic authority, even if that authority is centered on a bank or a shopping emporium. Only the largest office buildings still seek to overwhelm with architecture: they remain its last refuges. Buildings such as the AT&T Headquarters, 1986, by Philip Johnson, and the Humana Headquarters, 1986, by Michael Graves, are the last tragic monuments to an outdated, individualized capitalism.

We then find ourselves in cities where moments of order or reference are pasted onto otherwise nonsignificant interiors. Each of these gestures is of necessity incomplete. None of them really tells you about the building inside, or about the context: they do not condense and make visible what they are, how they are made, or what our relationship might be to them. They are often not even objects: their corners are eaten away by parking, they fit into preexisting walls, and they are contorted to gain more space by allowing unused pedestrian malls to pass in front of or through them. It is difficult to define their front doors, to decide their scale, or to figure out what their thin skin is made of. The imposition of American thought as unity has failed, because, except for its belief in the continuation of progress, of building, and of modernization, our society could not come to any agreement on that thought. The thin facades put up over the organization of natural resources, the true function of any building, last only long enough to sell that particular form of organization or consumption.

This is true of Europe as well as of America, and in fact, as the Western world continues its consumptive-colonizing march of the whole world. If one looks closer at America, it is only because it is here that architecture as the representation of the rational order of modernization was most clearly elucidated and built, just as the architecture of a purely bureaucratic order was defined best in France. And within America, it is wholly artificial cities such as Los Angeles that make the ultimate resistance to the architecture of absence visible.

At this point architecture is in retreat. Despite nostalgic attempts to reintroduce a former era in which human activity, the imposition of outside order, and built forms had a three-way relationship, we do not have an architecture in our urban environments (nor, increasingly outside of the urban/suburban configuration, either).[58] Nostalgic objects or urban experiences only reinforce the sense of architecture as a mask, a piece of physical advertising to be used to sell a particular set of services such as food or souvenirs.

Architecture survives in what Michel Foucault has called "heterotopias": cafes, railroad stations, rest homes, psychiatric clinics, prisons, cemeteries, theaters, museums, libraries, fairs.[59] Such places are in themselves "other," fragments of a utopian world floating in the real world, distorted mirrors of reality whose floor plans are maps for possible other worlds. These buildings share a characteristic of unreality. They are places for either very temporary or very permanent stays, rather than places of everyday activity, of production or consumption. Thus, "On the one hand, they perform the task of creating a space of illusion that reveals how all of real space is more illusionary, all the locations within which life is fragmented. On the other, they have the function of forming another space, another real space, as perfect, meticulous and well-arranged as ours is disordered, ill-conceived and in a sketchy state."[60] These are fragments of a utopia, the perfect world of architecture, realized according to the disjunctive and fragmenting rules of modernization.

Yet one could also say that architecture is indeed fulfilling the project of the modern. Many recent critics have attributed the current state of architecture, reduced to a producer of episodic fragments while desperately trying to find a realm of significance, to this condition. Anthony Vidler sees architecture as the last bulwark of a consciousness of the real world. According to him, "modernism," in formal terms...searched to replace wholes by the fragment, certainty by chance, temporality by atemporality, pyramidal composition by serial, unitarian structure by episodic. Modernism emerged by the mid-twenties as the dominant mode of all the arts – all, that is, except for architecture. Architecture, set apart by its socially functional ethic and its specific mode of production, alone rejected the overthrow of classical humanism implied by modernism and stood fast with all its contradictions as a *social* art [author's emphasis].[61]

Others have also argued for this special position that architecture has in the process of modernization. Mark Wigley asserts that architecture, as the privileged metaphor of Kantian metaphysics, is the unstable ground to a philosophical tradition based on that thinker's categorizations. When its reality, physicality, and its own reliance on Kantian idealism to justify its own existence is exposed, the whole structure will collapse. This Derridian notion reworks Marxist notions of the evil roots of a well-functioning capitalist system, however, and shares with Vidler a romanticization of architecture as something special.[62]

It is not. It is merely a part of culture as industry and as such has to come face to face with the same processes of modernization that have converted all arts into this industry. Its responses closely parallel the Faustian bargains of the other arts: in order to gain untold powers and riches, architecture becomes the perfect Speerian servant.[63] Fearing such a position, architecture retreats to realms it can invent, order, and project into the real world: other places, places of absence. In the end, the best that these buildings can do is "present the fact that the unpresentable exists."[64] The fact of the "unpresentability of the unpresent" is at the very heart of the modern dilemma, as the constant deferral of that which might satisfy us or produce meaning: it is the engine that keeps us productive and consumptive. It is our opium, that which gives a profoundly false, sterile, and tragic character to both modern society and its representation in cultural artifacts. Those artifacts can only confront us with a lack of meaning, or its presence in the absolute of death. They can make us aware of the lack of order, of the failure of the American dream and its architecture. They can show us the miasma of our urban environment, in which it is increasingly difficult to distinguish between the image of man, or machine, or man/machine according to which we live. With the creation of mass media, architecture cannot recreate us; it can only make us aware of our absence of self. It must allow us to live in a world of appearances, in other words, in a world made by man, the scene on which he appears and which makes him a member of humanity, and must make that world part of us.[65]

What then is to be done?

We must begin by understanding architecture as a critical investigation[66] and as an act of perception[67] that will allow us to remake a community in which we can mirror our humanity – a true unity: The remaking of the material of experience in the act of expression...is also a remaking of the experience of community[68] in the direction of greater order and community. At the same time, we must realize that, as we still live under the sign of modernization, this will be a modern project, or rather, the project of the modern: the projection of ourselves into the world perceived as technologically fragmented, inimical, violent and essentially destructive to our humanity. "The postmodern would be that which, in the modern, puts forward the unpresentable in presentation itself; that which denies itself the solace of good forms.... Let us wage war on totality; let us be witnesses to the unpresentable; let us activate the difference and save the honor of the name."[69] We must realize ourselves as satiric machines. In the past a possibility existed for a critical alternative to the urban scene – the bucolic or satyric landscape populated by the half-men and half-monsters whose dubious humanity rebelled against human culture. Our landscape is one of technology; its satyrs are robots. We must learn to inhabit this scene. A growing number of young designers are moving into the realm of the modern world. They are investigating the possibility of an architecture of empowerment, an appropriation of technology. This architecture will be a critical artifacting allowing us to break open the absent world and place us in a mapped and mirrored construction we identify as our world. Their constructions cannot be pure heterotopias, because such places cannot be stable objects. Instead, these designers plot strategies, deconstruct realities, and make.

1. Wright, Frank Lloyd. "The Art and Craft of the Machine." Lecture given to the Chicago Arts and Crafts Society, March 6, 1901. In: Kaufmann, Edgar and Ben Raeburn (Eds). *Frank Lloyd Wright: Writings and Buildings.* New York: New American Library, 1974 (1960), pp. 55-73, pp. 72-73.

2. Marx's compelling account of the development from tool to factory, though not wholly original, remained the succinct basis for countless later descriptions, seen as thrilling even to its most severe critics. Marx, Karl. *Capital. A Critique of Political Economy.* Ed. by Friedrich Engels. Transl. by Samuel Moore and Edward Aveling. New York: The Modern Library, 1906 (1867), pp. 405ff.

3. Marx, Karl, and Friedrich Engels. "Manifesto of the Communist Party." Feuer, Lewis S. (Ed). *Marx & Engels. Basic Writings on Politics and Philosophy.* New York: Anchor Books, 1959, pp. 6-41, p. 10. See also, for the most coherent critique of the history of such thinking in Western civilization: Berman, Marshall. *All That Is Solid Melts Into Air. The Experience of Modernity.* New York: Penguin Books, 1982.

4. *Wright*, p. 62

5. Ruskin, John. "The Two Paths is Art, Being lecture on Art, and its Application to Decoration and manufacture, Delivered in 1858-9." In:*The Works of John Ruskin, Volume XII.* New York: John Wiley & Sons, 1879; Stein, Roger B. *John Ruskin and Aesthetic Thought in America, 1840-1900.* Cambridge, MA: Harvard University Press, 1967.

6. Wright here recalls Victor Hugo's prediction, in *The Hunchback of Notre Dame*, that "this [the book] will kill that [the cathedral]." He sees a text-driven society opposing an image-driven one. *Wright*, p. 58

7. *Wright*, p. 69

8. *Wright*, p. 61.

9. To Wright, the machine is both the destroyer of conventional notions and the creator of a new, and democratic, world. Wright, p. 58.

10. Adams, Henry. *The Education of Henry Adams. An Autobiography.* Boston: Houghton Miflin Company, 1961 (1918), p. 343.

11. Trachtenberg, Alan. *The Incorporation of America. Culture & Society in the Gilded Age.* New York: Hill and Wang,1982, pp. 208-234.

12. For a description of the growth of corporate systems of control in America, see: Chandler, Alfred D. *The Visible Hand: The Managerial Revolution in American Business.* Cambridge, MA: Harvard University Press, 1977.

13. The Court of Honor was designed by a select group of leading architects under the leadership of Richard Morris Hunt. The figure of Columbia was the work of Frederick William MacMonnies. For views of the Fair, see: Applebaum, Stanley. *The Chicago World's Fair of 1893. A Photographic Record.* New York: Dover Publications, Inc., 1980.

14. Van Brunt was a past President of the American Institute of Architects and a leader in debates on what should constitute an American style of architecture (he argued for a modernized classicism). Coles, William A. *Architecture and Society. Selected Essays of Henry Van Brunt.* Cambridge, MA: The Belknap Press of Harvard University Press, 1969.

15. Cf. T.J. Jackson Lears. *No Place of Grace. Antimodernism and the Transformation of American Culture 1880-1920.* New York: Pantheon Books, 1981.

16. For summaries of the development of this peculiar brand of classicism, see either: Wilson, Richard Guy. "The Great Civilization." Wilson, Richard Guy (Ed.).*The American Renaissance 1876-1917.* New York: Pantheon Books, 1979, pp. 11-74; or: Stern, Robert A.M. "Stages of Metropolitanism." Stern, Robert A.M., Gregory Gilmartin and John Montague Massengale. *New York 1900. Metropolitan Architectrue and Urbanism 1890-1915.* New York: Rizzoli International Publciations, 1983, pp. 10-25.

17. The American Institute of Architecture was founded in 1851, specifically to define the profession to the exclusion of self-trained men, immigrant carpenter/builders and women designers. These efforts led to the setting up of state boards of architecture and to the passing of national legislation defining the profession in 1897. See: Wright, Gwendolyn. *Moralism and the Model Home: Domestic Architecture and Cultural Conflict in Chicago, 1873-1913.* Chicago: The University of Chicago Press, 1980.

18. Three excellent descriptions of this process can be found in *The American City from the Civil War to the New Deal* (Transl. by Barbara Luigia La Penta; London: Granada Publishing, 1980 (1973)): "Toward an "Imperial City:" Daniel H. Burnham and the City Beautiful Movement," by Maria Manieri-Elia (pp. 1-142); "From Parks to the Region: Progressive Ideology and the Reform of the American City," by Francesco Dal Co (pp. 143-292); and "The Disenchanted Mountain: The Skyscraper and the City," by Manfredo Tafuri (pp. 389-528).

19. A licensed architect in Holland, Germany and Switzerland must have an engineering degree.

20. Singelenberg, Pieter. *H.P. Berlage. Idea and Style. The Quest for Modern Architecture.* Utrecht: Haentjes Dekker & Gumbert, 1972; Polano, Sergio. *Hendrik Petrus Berlage; Complete Works.* New York: Rizzoli International Publications, 1988; Wiekart, K. *J.J.P. Oud.* Amsterdam: Meulenhoof, 1965.

21. "Landscape" derives from the Dutch "landschap"—signifying a "made" or "created" land, rather than one that is "natural."

22. Mondrian, Piet. "The Realization of Neo-plasticism in the Distant Future and in Architecture Today." *De Stijl*, Volume 5. #3, pp. 41-47.

23. Ibid, p. 165

24. This development mirrors those in the political arena, where idealistic bourgeois communists and others proposed unrealizable utopian solutions after a total revolution, while social democrats tended towards the efficient renovation of bourgeois capitalism.

25. K. Michael Hays, however, makes the case that here Meyer "injects into bourgeois humanist normality the alienating dissonances and contradictions that characterize rapid industrialization..." and that the League of Nations projects points to the "processes of its making." A close reading of the drawings, however, fails to convey that these otherwise laudable objectives are indeed carried out. Hays, K. Michael. "Reproduction and Negation: The Cognitive Project of the Avant-Garde." In: Colomina, Beatriz (Ed.) *Architecture Reproduction.* New York: Princeton Architectural Press, 1988, pp. 153-179, p. 153, p. 158.

26. Van Doesburg did venture into the realm of architecture, or "space constructions," - but this was after his break with Mondrian. The best documentation in the English language on debates between architects and painters in the De Stijl group may be found in Troy, Nancy J. *The De Stijl Environment.* Cambridge, MA: The MIT Press, 1983.

27. Bless, Frits. *Rietveld 1888-1964. Een Biografie.* Amsterdam: Uitgeverij Bert Bakker, 1982.

28. Most succinctly by Manfredo Tafuri in *Architecture and Utopia. Design and Capitalist Development.* Transl. by Barbara Luigia La Penta. Cambridge, MA: The MIT Press, 1979 (1973).

29. Cf. Williams, Raymond. *Culture and Society, 1780-1950.* New York: Harper and Row, 1966.

30. The problem might be traced back to the distinction between the liberating potential of revolutions, and the need to base freedom and empowerment on a constitution. Architectural revolutionaries never became founders of a constructive and liberating architectural construct, at least in Western Europe. Cf. Arendt, Hannah. *On Revolution.* New York: Viking Press, 1963.

31. Marinetti, F.T. "The Foundation and Manifesto of Futurism." First published in *Le Figaro*, February 20, 1909. Transl. by Joshua C. Taylor. In: Chipp, Hershel B. *Theories of Modern Art. A Source Book by Artists and Critics.* Berkeley, CA: University of California Press, 1968, pp. 285-289, p. 286.

32. Sant'Elia, Antonio, and F. T. Marinetti. "Futurist Architecture." First published in July, 1916. Transl. by Michael Bullock. In: Conrads, Ulrich (Ed.) *Programs and Manifestoes on 20th-Century Architecture.* Cambridge, MA: The MIT Press, 1970 (1964). pp. 34-40, p. 35.

33. Ibid, p. 37.

34. Ibid.

35. Cf. *Marinetti*, p. 288.

36. Cf. Celant, Germano. *Unexpressionism. Art Beyond the Contemporary.* Transl. by Joachim Neugroschel. New York: Rizzoli International Publications, 1988.

37. Much of the theory of current practice is an adaptation of Derridian textual analysis to the making of art. See, for instance Ulmer, Gregory. "The Object of Post-criticism." In: Foster, Hal (Ed) *The Anti-Aesthetic. Essays on Postmodern Culture.* Port Townsend, WA: Bay Press, 1983, pp. 83-110.

38. Levi-Strauss, Claude. "The Science of the Concrete." Levi-Strauss, Claude. The *Savage Mind.* Chicago: The University of Chicago Press, 1966 (1962), pp. 1-34.

39. Ibid, pp. 161ff.

40. Duchamp, Marcel. "The Bride Stripped Bare by Her Bachelors, Even." Transl. by George Heard Hamilton. In: Lippard, Lucy (Ed.). *Dadas on Art.* Englewood, N.J.: Prentice-Hall, Inc., 1971, pp. 144-154

41. "The Rise and Fall of the City of Mahoganny," Baden-Baden, July 17, 1927; "The Threepenny Opera," Berlin, August 31, 1928.

42. For the differences between rationalism, suprematism, productivism and constructivism, among the various variations on post-revolutionary constructive art, see: Khan-Magomedov, Selim O. *Pioneers of Soviet Architecture. The Search for New Solutions in the 1920s and 1930s*. Transl. by Alexander Lieven. New York: Rizzoli International Publications, 1987 (1983).

43. Beeren, Wim A.L. *Kazimir Malevich*. Amsterdam: Stedelijk Museum Amsterdam, 1989.

44. El Lissitzky. *Russia: An Architecture for World Revolution*. Transl. by Eric Dluhosch. Cambridge, MA: The MIT Press, 1984 (1930).

45. Khan-Magomedov. (1983), pp. 106ff.

46. Gozak, Andrei and Andrei Leonidov. *Ivan Leonidov: The Complete Works*. Transl. by Catherine Cook et.al. New York: Rizzoli International Publications, Inc., 1988, pp. 43-49.

47. *Gozak*, p. 12.

48. Ibid, pp. 105-117.

49. Kahn-Magomedov, Selim O. *Rodchenko: The Complete Work*. Transl. by Hugh Evans. Cambridge, MA: The MIT Press, 1987.

50. Martin, Jean Hubert, et.al. *Man Ray Photographs*. New York: Thames and Hudson, 1982; Janus. *Man Ray; The Photographic Image*. Translated by Murtha Baca. Woodbury, NY: Barrons Press, 1980; Krauss, Rosalind, and Jane Livingston. *L'Amour Fou: Photography and Surrealism*. New York: Abbeville Press, 1985; Rose, Barbara. "Kinetic Solutions to Pictorial Problems: The Films of Man Ray and Moholy-Nagy." *Artforum* 10, September, 1971, pp. 68-73.

51. Haus, Andreas. *Moholy-Nagy, Photographs and Photograms*. Transl. by Frederic Samson. New York: Pantheon Books, 1980; Hight, Eleanor. *Moholy-Nagy: Photography and Film in Weimar Germany*; Wellesley, MA: Wellesley College Museum, 1985.

52. Benjamin, Walter. "The Work of Art in the Age of Mechanical Reproduction." Transl by Harry Zohn. In: Benjamin, Walter. *Illuminations*. New York: Schocken Books, 1969., pp. 217-251, p. 236

53. Baudrillard, Jean. *Simulations*. Transl. by Paul Foss, Paul Patton and Philip Beitchman. New York: Semiotext(e), Inc., 1983, p. 143.

54. Hines, Thomas S. *Burnham of Chicago. Architect and Planner*. Chicago: The University of Chicago Press, 1979 (1974), pp.312ff.

55. Hines, Thomas S. *Richard Neutra and the Search for Modern Architecture. A Biography and History*. New York: Oxford University Press, 1982, pp. 60ff.

56. Wright, Frank Lloyd. *The Living City*. New York: Horizon Press, 1958.

57. Tafuri, op.cit., p. 181.

58. Cornell West has pointed out the failure of the American Dream in its attempt to impose an order of significance on society, and has also pointed out that the nostalgic dreams of such an order are in fact extensions of the colonizing and dis-empowering efforts of the capitalist system. Cornel West, Lecture given at the Southern California Institute of Architecture, Santa Monica, California, March 28, 1988.

59. Foucault, Michel. "Other Spaces. The Principles of Heterotopia." *Lotus* #48/49, 1986, p. 14ff.

60. Foucault, p. 17.

61. Vidler, Anthony. "Commentary." *Oppositions* #9, Summer, 1977, pp. 37-41.

62. Wigley, Mark. "Postmortem Architecture: The Taste of Derrida." *Perspecta* 23, pp. 156-172.

63. Cf. Berman, pp. 60-71.

64. Lyotard, Jean-Francois. *The Postmodern Condition: A Report on Knowledge*. Transl. by Geoff Bennington and Brian Masuri. Minneapolis: University of Minnesota Press, 1984 (1979), p. 78.

65. Cf. Arendt, Hannah. *The Life of the Mind. Thinking*. New York: Harcourt Brace Jovanovich, 1978, pp. 19ff. This thought is picked up by Svetlana Alpers, who claims that Dutch art of the seventeenth century accomplished much of this goal. Alpers, Svetlana. "Seeing as Knowing: A Dutch Connection."

66. Colomina, Beatriz. "Introduction: On Architecture, Production and Reproduction." *Architecture Reproduction*, op.cit., pp. 7-23, p. 17.

67. Dewey, John. *Art as Experience*. New York: Perigree Books, 1980 (1934), p. 47.

68. Ibid, p. 81.

69. *Lyotard*, op.cit., p. 78, p. 82.

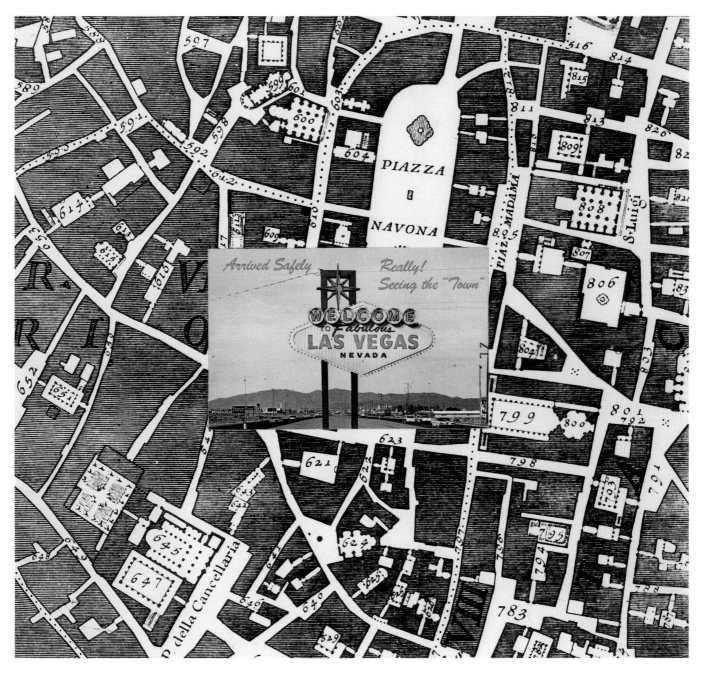

VENTURI,
SCOTT BROWN
& IZENOUR
detail from
Weclome to Fabulous
Las Vegas Nevada /Nolli's
Map of Rome;
Learning from Las Vegas
Cambridge, Massachusetts, 1972

FOUR GODFATHERS

Robert Venturi stands at the beginning of the postmodern era. In what has come to be known as a Jencksian postmodern movement,[1] Venturi is now associated with attempts to make architecture a defensive bulwark of meaning clothed in classical garb. Initially, Venturi was the savior of the project of the modern. He understood that the object could no longer be fetishized as a hierarchical and unitary signifier of function, imposing an *a priori* order on all activities it served. He instead argued for a new kind of design, one acknowledging electronic communication as the basis of the latest cycle of production and consumption, and attempting to critically harness this means of control.

Venturi first exposed the fact that architecture was not keeping pace with the increased complexity and contradiction of the modern world. He also pointed out that its formal vocabulary could not yet represent such complexities. Already, in his 1966 *Complexity and Contradiction in Architecture*,[2] Venturi questioned the efficacy of the traditional monument and the subjection of function to any supposed cultural agreement or signification. In *Learning from Las Vegas*, Venturi wrote: "But complex programs and settings require complex combinations of media beyond the purer architectural triad of structure, form, and light at the service of space. They suggest an architecture of bold communication rather than one of subtle expression."[3] He described a landscape of a scale immeasurable in traditional architectural terms, lacking clear boundaries by the day,[4] entirely boundless by night.[5] It was a landscape ordered by chaos,[6] and continually changing.[7] Its only reality, the only thing in which money was invested and the only noticeable feature, was the sign.[8] Modern reality had reduced itself to freefloating signs, advertisements for shows. Traditional definitions of reality and (its) space had disappeared. Making all this possible was a great deal of artifacting. Because the landscape was treated as a tabula rasa, building shells, air conditioning, lighting, sewage, and all the other technological miracles allowing us to inhabit that inimical place needed to be constructed. Venturi pointed out that all of these man-made artifacts were essentially invisible, abstract and recessive. You could not understand the order of the space by understanding how it had been made and how it functioned. The signs only advertise societal games ritualized as architecture by a culture incapable of defining its own physical representation.

Until the mid-70s, Venturi tried to realize architecturally this brilliant analysis, developed for the extreme case of Las Vegas, but applicable to the chaotic landscape and ritualized activities of suburbs and exurbs all around the world. Projects such as the Football Hall of Fame for New Brunswick, New Jersey, 1967, proposed an antidote to the closed monument by creating a purposefully uncomfortable and unfinished form: a building that was a bleacher on one side, and on the other side only the scaffolding for a sign. The interior's nave-like space was an episodic trail of scaleless, electronically produced images and fragmentary displays.[9] Venturi argued for an architecture of pure communication, a non-material manipulation of experience.

Architecture could function similarly to television or advertising, but in an even more complete and critical manner.[10] Irony was the chosen tool: "Irony (not cynical comment on the 'status quo') is the artist's gentle subversion."[11] Venturi and Brown's method

VENTURI, RAUCH
& SCOTT BROWN
interior perspective collage
National College
Football Hall of Fame
Competition Project
1967

used decorative and repetitive patterns. According to them, this strategy appropriated and subverted the essential character of mass-consumption goods. If architecture was no more than an advertisement of goods, it should reveal itself by (gently) commenting on these characteristics. "Repetitive patterns can accommodate the standardization that is typical of our industrial construction methods.... Buildings whose structural and spatial systems are obfuscated by an allover appliqué of patterned and representational mosaics and frescoes serve as exemplars to us in our efforts to achieve richness of effect with today's methods and materials."[12] In the end, this gentle irony became only a comforting witticism. In turn it too disappeared, in favor of an architecture meant to serve efficiently while "enriching" our lives – masking the absence of meaning with a decorative pattern that, in its appliqué of classical elements, increasingly perpetuates the status quo.

VENTURI, RAUCH
& SCOTT BROWN
sections, elevation
National College
Football Hall of Fame
Competition Project
1967

At one point Venturi stated: "I sometimes think my next text should be called Modern Architecture is Almost Alright."[13] Instead this dictum became the battle cry of a group of late modernists centered around those whom **Peter Eisenman** called the "New York Five."[14] For them, modernism, in its very self-consciousness as a style, comments on and furthers the process of modernization. Eisenman, the theoretician of the movement, transported this romantic rhetoric into a much darker and more ambivalent territory by using Noam Chomsky's syntactical model, and other theories of communication.[15] Over a ten year period, starting in 1967, Eisenman annually produced a house which textually manipulated architectural elements. For him, meaning generates from syntactical relationships among structural systems.

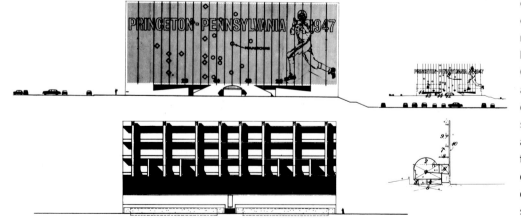

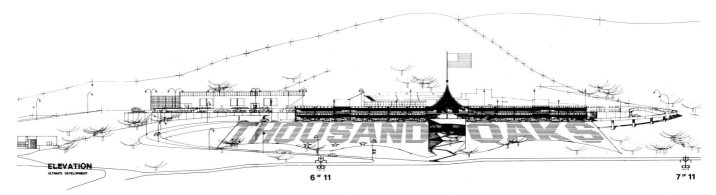

Functional attributes are literal analogies for those invisible structures of signification ordering our lives. This analog is created by the juxtaposition of several contradictory systems of syntactical relationships, carefully coded as abstract structures, instead of by the perception of their functional attributes, such as the admission of people (doors) or light (windows). He attempts to give that which remains hidden a three dimensional form, allowing us to experience the abstract structure of order we partake in, but never fully understand. The irreducible structure sought by modernists revealed itself in neutral white, denuded of function, and exposing – in good Heisenbergian fashion – the tendency of a complete system to reveal its essential incompleteness. The project of the modern was pushed to its extreme – an uninhabitable utopia constructed and positioned on the landscape.[16]

The culmination and turning point of this architecture was the unrealized, but well documented, project for House X.[17] Eisenman set out to expose the incompleteness of any "perfect" system, and to build a new order out of this very incompleteness. The design refused to allow the suburban house to deny the technological and socio-economic basis of its operation. In keeping with the rigid geometric tradition underlying all formal architectural manipulations, Eisenman selected the "L" as his, necessarily both compound and incomplete, generating shape. By inverting, making three-dimensional, intersecting, and otherwise manipulating this basic shape, Eisenman generated a conglomeration of enclosed and implied shapes occupying an ex-urban site. In a self-conscious parody of a reasoned decision-making process, the "architect-as-deranged scientist/bureaucrat" made decisions denying the

VENTURI, RAUCH & SCOTT BROWN
elevation from freeway
Thousand Oaks Civic Center Competition Project
Thousand Oaks, California, 1969

PETER EISENMAN
axonometric diagram
House VI/Frank Residence
Washington, Connecticut, 1975

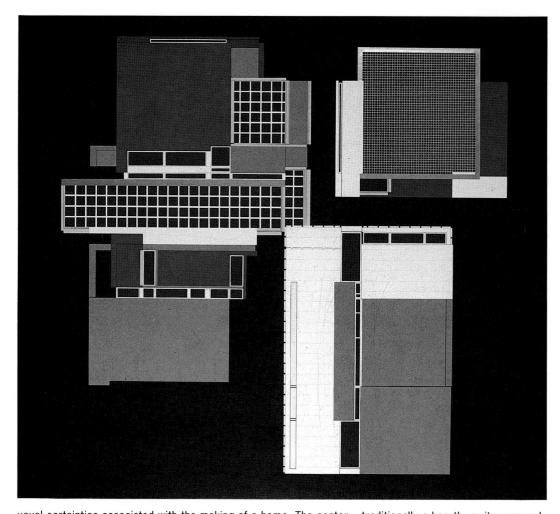

usual certainties associated with the making of a home. The center – traditionally a hearth, or its manmade equivalent – electrical, telephone and sewage grids – was replaced by an uninhabitable void. Stable horizon lines and anything allowing one to understand the ground plane were also absent, as was a clear understanding of interior and exterior boundaries. The net result of all of these operations was a machine made operable by the complete removal of all natural forces. It thus frustrated perception and preconceptions of function and facade representation. This "anti-architecture," of course, could not be built. Eisenman described his operation as archaeology, an investigation into absurd systems of order underlying our everyday lives. He simultaneously exposed their contradictions, and revealed the essential instability of our notions of home, belonging, and humanity. The house is positioned as a critique of humanism.

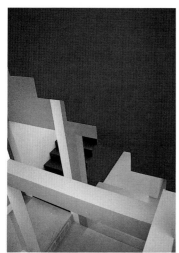

According to Mario Gandelsonas' introduction to the volume describing this investigation,[18] Eisenman has performed a sacrifice, a ritualized burial of humanistic architecture allowing for an undefined other to emerge. That other seems to be the modern, defined by Eisenman as the condition of absence. Eisenman's career has subsequently mapped out this terrain through a process of denial and erasure. By digging away at what we consider to be controllable ways of thinking and doing, Eisenman hopes to unveil the void at the heart of our activities. Tracing what has been erased or built over brings into focus the inner contradictions of our actions and their basis in denial. Recent projects make more

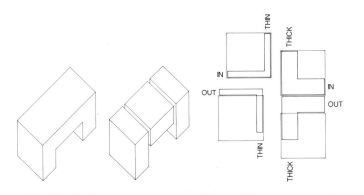

PETER EISENMAN
evolution diagram
House X
1979

explicit attempts to represent scientific processes, replacing humanistically based thought-processes with Zen-like theories of uncertainty, indeterminacy, dissipation, and chaos. Eisenman and other architects are acknowledging science's revelation of the project of the modern's ultimate ground as the denial of the individual as an experiencing, definable being. Eisenman documents this process of scientific thought as it engenders a technology characterizing the modern world. If followed to its logical conclusion, it culminates in a self-destruction that is not merely theoretical, for it also implicates the atom bomb, World War II death camps, and genetic engineering, as well as the destruction of the very concept of nature defining our world.

Eisenman has become the leader of a large group that wishes to feed the data produced by processes of modernization back into the system, hoping that

these representational feedback loops will foreground self-destruction. Other than the fact that such a process leads to the death of architecture, of architects, of selves, the result is not clear.

What remains could be a making, or an artifacting beyond mere self destruction – a possibility one of Eisenman's more talented disciples, Daniel Libeskind, hints at (*see Chapter 3*).

PETER EISENMAN
axonometric model
House X
1979
Photo: Dick Frank

In the work of Daniel Libeskind, Eisenman's influence intersects with that of John Hejduk. Another member of the New York Five, Hejduk also explores architecture as a language. Hejduk is less interested in the formal characteristics of language, favoring the narrative qualities inherent in the making and experience of buildings. Hejduk's main task, diligently pursued over the last twenty years, is to eliminate elements defining architecture in "technological" terms, i.e., as part of a logical and closed system reaffirming the known world. Space as "an autonomous geometrical projection" is replaced by its "lived form";[19] function is replaced by the telling of a story. This activity can open up a passage beyond the visible world, enabling man to confront the nature of technology and its roots in the extension of the self into the world. This process simultaneously remakes the world and absorbs the self. Hejduk is a chronicler, sometimes

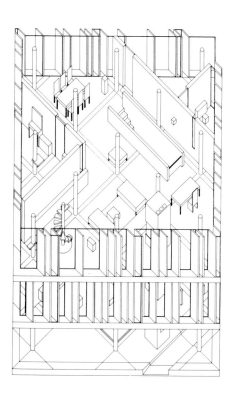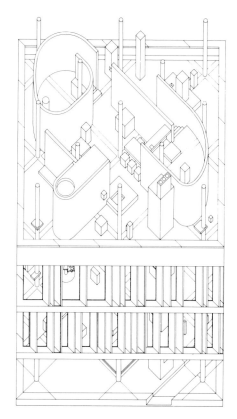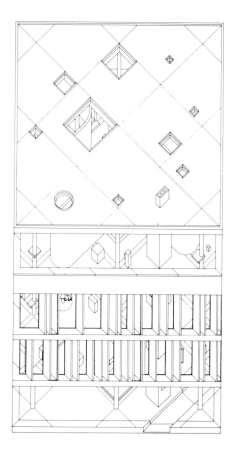

JOHN HEJDUK
projections
Diamond House A
1964

nostalgic, sometimes messianic, of the loss of self and of the world of technology, who proposes a counterpoint: poesis. His proposal offers an alternate world in which the making of architecture is the most essential social act, and the architect is a storyteller or shaman.

Hejduk's position, fully developed in his masque series begun in 1979, reduces architecture to a two-dimensional implosion of composition. In buildings such as the Diamond Houses and Diamond Museum of 1963-1967, he literally "squeezes" space and function out of proposals resembling, on a surface level, Eisenman's work of the same period. He then abandoned the certainties of geometry, and the idea that architecture could impose a preexisting order. Starting with the Wall House in 1968, he proposed biomorphic forms that bypass

attempts at definition and lack any clear front, back, top or bottom, and then set them against the division of a wall. This wall created a landscape, a made piece of land, by arbitrarily marking a division in the natural world. The wall merely announces a human act, and proposes an arena for action on one of its sides. That arena was filled with the masque projects over the following years.[20] These masques, unlike their sixteenth- and seventeenth-century counterparts, are not directly allegorical, nor do they affirm calibrated positions of power, staged in a series of measured compositions.[21] Rather, they reveal the potential actions or roles that architecture can invent. The masques are collected fragments of architecture: towers, walls, cones, cylinders, or triangles, floating in an undifferentiated field. There is neither stage nor script, only form. Coherence and narrative develop in this assemblage of composite form. In some cases triangular forms are intersected by cones; in others there

may be kidney-shapes with long tubes protruding. They all are unclassifiable in terms of traditional function, scale or context. These crafted and often movable masques are proposals for activities or people lacking any existence outside of their own realm: Wind Tower, Hedge Walk, The Bargeman, Arbitration Hall, and most pregnantly, the Mask of Medusa. This myth contains hope, but danger and foreboding as well. If one confronts the monstrous alternative to a safe reality, one could turn into stone.

Rather than collecting these places and people into a coherent narrative, Hejduk proposes vignettes intimating both a larger narrative and a larger society. In the Berlin Masque of 1983, the most complete of these proposals, a city's destruction by a

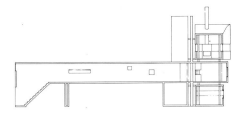

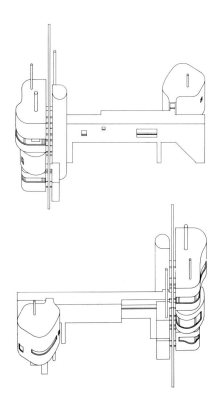

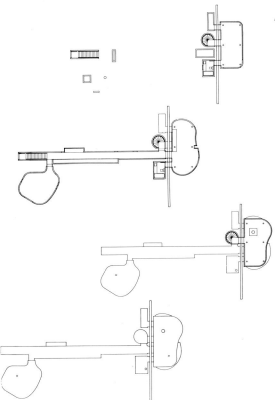

JOHN HEJDUK
section, projections and plans
Wall House/Bye House
Ridgefield, Connecticut, 1973

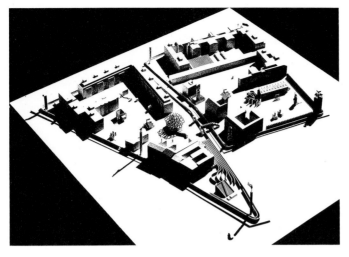

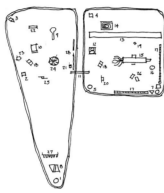

HEDGES 12'-0" HIGH SURROUND ENTIRE SITE

JOHN HEJDUK
model, plan
Berlin Masque
Berlin, Germany, 1982

rational political elongation of technology is posed and then solved by a proposed small community in which inhabitants are defined by an architecture that both represents and houses them. The coherence is guaranteed by an architecture about social acts, for there is neither a center, nor a periphery, monuments, or any housing – only the act of arbitration, the measuring of the wind, the selling of clothes.

Hejduk's projects are mythological proposals for a world that may have been in the past, may exist in the present, might exist in the future, or perhaps is in a state of becoming. Their images remind us of forms we may have known, as do the forms of the Midwest of the 1920s, of the Lancaster/Hannover Masque, 1983,[22] or they propose futuristic visions. On every level, they present an alternative affirmation of our world. Hejduk proposes alter-

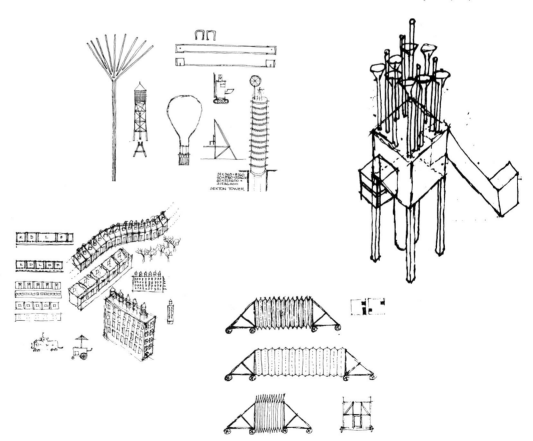

JOHN HEJDUK
elements
Lancaster/Hannover Masque
1983

JOHN HEJDUK
elements
Berlin Masque
Berlin, Germany, 1982

FRANK GEHRY
O'Neill Haybarn
San Juan Capistrano, California,
1968

nate ways of disciplining and physically organizing our daily activities so that they can have significance. Our cities and societies need not be centers and structures of authority, but fragments of coalition and communal research. A technology embodying the dissolution of the self into the act of making, could replace the division between the self and world. Finally, the architect himself is caught up in this act, and becomes a mask, a poet and a poseur.

A myth of the death of self and resurrection of the human act of making is unrealizable – for to build these structures would turn them into objects, although Hejduk has done just that in a few compromised buildings in Berlin. Their construction is their death: they are tombstones for the self and our society. Any alternative, mythological world can only exist outside of our lived experience. If, as Daniel Libeskind claims, "a space of passage"[23] is opened up, its threshold cannot be crossed, precisely because the space is not physical. But Hejduk opens up this space in language by telling us stories, not necessarily about ourselves, and not necessarily hoping that we believe them, but as his faithful act of building, of constructing a possible other world.

Frank Gehry concerns himself with building in the real world. Unlike Venturi, Eisenman, and Hejduk, Gehry mines and remakes the existing world. There is little theory in his work, and much of what he proposes gets built. Gehry's architecture presents a possible mode of working in the world that reveals its underlying forms and fantasies. In contrast to his East coast contemporaries, Gehry's career is not based on an exploration of the liberating possibilities inherent in architecture's formal characteristics. Gehry's career confronts us with a completely different impulse at the heart of modernism. As carried out by the most radical functionalists and abstractionists, whether in the De Stijl group, in Russia, or at the Bauhaus, this rigorous pursuit to do away with all excess baggage represents an effort to eliminate cultural signification. Any element added to the purely structural or functional requirements of a building, argued diverse designers such as Le Corbusier and El Lissitzky, only recalls monuments of the past and thus fetters any liberated perception. Space is purposefully undefined, challenging the senses rather than defining perimeters of construction. Context was seen as imprisoning; scale suggestions should not restrict a building. Functional constraints should only indicate a completely flexible arrangement as markers for a new world, rather than be seen as a rigid set of givens: "Thus *Proun* supersedes painting and its artists on the one hand, the machine and the engineer on the other, and proceeds to the construction of space, organizing them [sic] through material elements in all dimensions and builds a new, manifold, yet unified image of man."[24] Columns, window surrounds, imposed symmetries and other compositional hierarchies impede the working of the building as a mechanism of continual change, an integral part of the continual work of

FRANK GEHRY
Gehry Residence
Santa Monica, California, 1978

FRANK GEHRY
kitchen
Gehry Residence
Santa Monica, California, 1978

society. The process of modernization itself demands ever greater abstraction.

Gehry's reach extends beyond the false roadblock of functional-ism, spatial fetishism, and contextualism to the completely free manipulation of building material. Influenced by painters and sculptors of 1950s and 1960s, Carl André in particular, Gehry situates architecture in the realm of pure gesture (for example, the O'Neil Hay Barn of 1968), or as an act of uncovering. Paradoxically, he simultaneously rediscovered the physicality of building while moving from reduction and revealing to an affirmation of the activity of building, and an abstraction of that revelation into enigmatic, scaleless objects remapping the world. A mythology was created, proposing an alternate world as a physical extension of everyday reality.

Gehry first removed the protective skin from the building, exposing its descriptive anatomy. Then he altered all points of the building characteristic of a closed object. The most famous example of this strategy is his own house, completed in 1978. Interior walls of a pre-existing house, to which he added a U-shaped addition, were stripped, revealing wood studs and the electrical conduits snaking through them. From the outside, portions of the facade were removed, and glass was placed over the internal structure. Pre-existing windows were left hanging in front of the wall, sometimes as mirrors. In the addition, functional boxes gave way to a flowing space defined

FRANK GEHRY
plan
Sirmai-Petersen Residence
Thousand Oaks, California, 1985

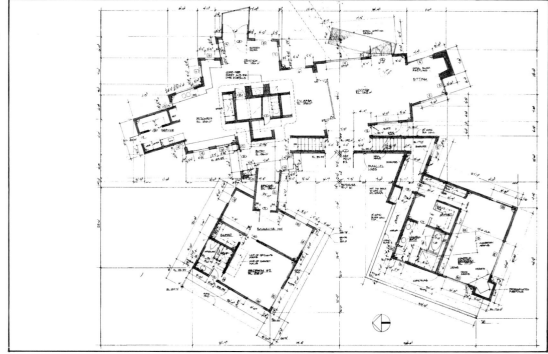

by an asphalt floor, a corner was replaced by a distorted glass insert, and a tumbling cube – one of Lissitzky's *prouns* – crashed into the kitchen area. The house confounds any traditional sense of composition, facade, scale or plan; yet, it is made of recognizable materials, which provide an internal scale and which unearth the original craft of the house. One discovers how the building is *made*, rather than how it is *used* or which social class it represents. Gehry then added building elements usually cast out of architecture, but essential to the act of building: concrete formwork, chainlink fencing, and corrugated metal. These elements integrated his buildings into a context of seemingly disconnected elements organized by one's continually changing perception.

Gehry's building designs are perfectly modern. As part of the chaotic field of a modern metropolis, they only represent the act of making, and are thus vulnerable to continual growth and decay. As ephemeral markers they designate the self-effacing path architecture takes as it articulates everyday life in the age of modernization. The end point of architecture and art, they suggest, is not one of reductive abstraction, but one of merging architecture and the physical world. In this process, the architect's role becomes one of asserting how perception, knowing, and making interact to deform and re-form reality.

After establishing this working method in the mid-1970s, Gehry then developed two further strategies: "pavilionizing" and cutting, or "Matta-Clarking." The first of these strategies is evident in his proposed addition of 1981 to a house he had designed twenty years earlier. Here, the exterior is broken up into discrete objects, each with a strong sculptural shape, color, and material, which make no direct reference to function, context, or the spatial volume inside, which in fact flows throughout all of these objects. In his house projects, culminating in the Sirmai-Peterson House of 1987, and the Winton Guest House of 1988, this abstraction of built form into enigmatic shapes has paradoxically led to the combination of a flowing interior space of the modern suburban home, liberated by technology, with a monumentality that makes these houses seem both strange and public, and similar to Hejduk's masque objects in their mythological tone.

The pavilionizing in his public buildings led to a new monumentality that can hazard direct references to classical elements, as is the case in the Loyola Law

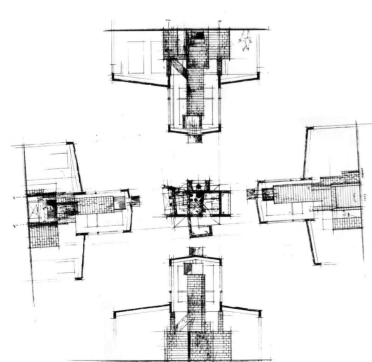

FRANK GEHRY
sections, plan,
Central Fireplace Object
Sirmai-Petersen Residence
Thousand Oaks, California, 1985

FRANK GEHRY
Winton Guest House
Wayzata, Minnesota, 1988
Photo: Mark Darley

GORDON MATTA-CLARK
House Splitting
Englewood, New Jersey, 1974
Photo: Adam Reich

School of 1985. For Gehry, such references are fragments of a spatial and temporal cultural continuum organizing objects in the School's courtyards as if they were props on a stage set. In the main building at Loyola, as in buildings such as the Yale Psychiatric Institute, 1989, or the Herman Miller Western Distribution Facility, 1989, function and the delimitation of space are literally relegated to the background. Against these backdrops, with their own scale and articulation, but not constructed as inherently stable or attention-grabbing monuments, the pavilions signify the most important activity of the

FRANK GEHRY
courtyard
Loyola Law School
Los Angeles, California, 1986

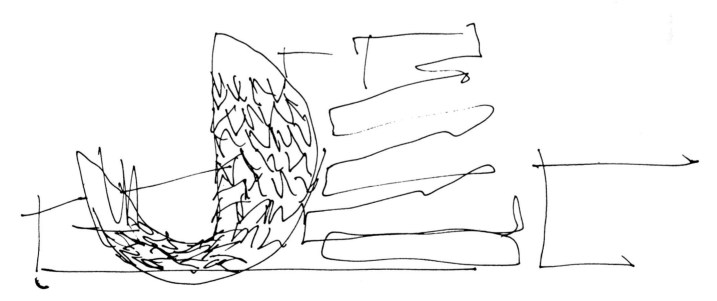

FRANK GEHRY
study
Fishdance Restaurant
Kobe, Japan, 1987

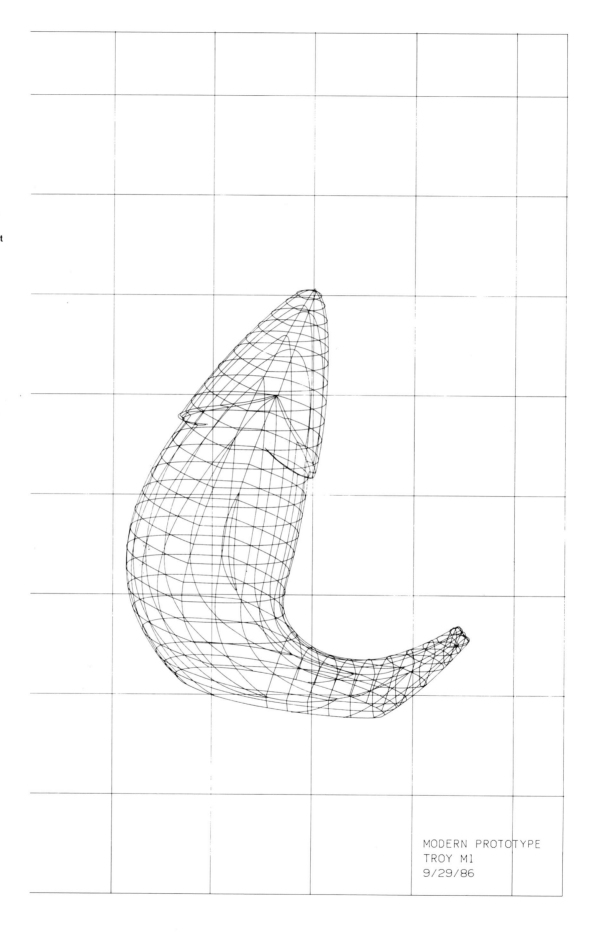

MODERN PROTOTYPE
TROY MI
9/29/86

building: what Gehry calls the client's fantasy about the nature of the program and site.[25]

Architecture becomes the actual construction of an alternative world composed of building blocks in the world around us. It thus reveals the inherent coherence of the program and the context, as well as of the building materials. In order to emphasize this revelation, Gehry has borrowed the tactics of the artist Gordon Matta-Clark, who ripped open existing buildings and, in the act of revelation, exposed implied shapes (circles, spirals, lozenges) in the space opened up.[26]

Gehry shows that the act of building can, beyond affirming itself as the staging of possible activities escaping what is known, capture the unknowable. He furthers this act by employing his favorite fish and snake forms.

The fish is a private emblem, a childhood memory, and also an allusive form. It tends towards shapes, like Eisenman's L, but is none of them. Its parabolic curve implies infinitude. Gehry has described this object as a Zen *koan* of perfection. Yet this perfection also has a figurative shape, that of a fish, a strange monster invading the city. More recently Gehry has sublimated these elements into more abstract and fragmented expres-

FRANK GEHRY
model
Walt Disney Concert Hall
Los Angeles, California, 1988
Photo: Tom Bonner

sions, as in the Disney Concert Hall proposal of 1988, thus integrating the unknowable into the city's texture.

Gehry suggests the possibility that building must of necessity be fragmented, enigmatic, and assembled as a stage for human action, and that it must also continue the search for perfection through both abstraction and "strangemaking," and through an active reworking of the world. Gehry recognizes neither objects nor contexts, perceivers nor a perceptible extended world, only the continually changing act of making and knowing, connected by the thin, and perhaps idiosyncratic, thread of the artifacting of the world.

Venturi, Eisenman, Hejduk and Gehry have all developed significant strategies for the continuation of the project of the modern. The constellation of activities they have proposed question how one might represent processes of modernization and realize them in physical form. It is no longer a matter of creating closed objects that stand for what our society is already, or could be. Rather, they propose that architecture as an activity can best be understood as process, communication, staging, or crafting, as an activity allowing the self to be constituted in the remaking of the world. These are essentially social activities that extend the self into the public realm. They are also fantastic projections, in the sense that they can never be fully realized without defeating themselves. Their proposals for an architecture beyond function, space or context have opened up the field.

1. Charles Jencks gave a name and particular character to the movement in his *The Language of Post-Modern Architecture*, first published in 1977 (London: Academy Editions). This book has since been followed by variations on the same theme, attempting to rescue Post-Modern architecture from a tradition affirming humanism and the status quo.

2. Venturi, Robert. *Complexity and Contradiction in Architecture.* New York: The Museum of Modern Art, 1966.

3. Venturi, Robert, Denise Scott Brown, and Steven Izenour. *Learning From Las Vegas: The Forgotten Symbolism of Architectural Form.* Cambridge, MA: The MIT Press, 1977 (1972), p. 9.

4. Ibid, p. 50.

5. Ibid, p. 49.

6. Ibid, p. 20.

7. Ibid, p. 34.

8. Ibid, p. 8.

9. Venturi, Robert. "A Bildingboard Involving Movies, Relics and Space." Architectural Forum, April 1968. Reprinted in Venturi, Robert and Denise Scott Brown's *A View from the Campidoglio. Selected Essays 1953-1984.* New York: Harper & Row, Publishers, 1984, pp. 14-18.

10. Venturi. *Complexity and Contradiction,* pp. 102-3.

11. Brown, Denise Scott. "Pop Off: Reply to Kenneth Frampton." Casabella, December, 1971. *View,* pp. 34-37, p. 36.

12. Venturi, Robert. "The RIBA Annual Discourse" (1981). *View,* pp. 104-107, p.105.

13. Venturi, Robert. "Learning the Right Lessons from the Beaux-Arts." *Architectural Design*, Volume 49, #1, 1979, pp. 23-31, p. 23.

14. The name of this group derives from the book *Five Architects* (Peter Eisenman et.al. New York: Wittenborn & Company, 1972).

15. Chomsky, Noam. *Syntactic Structures.* The Hague: Mouton Publishers, 1968; *Aspects of the Theory of Syntax.* Cambridge, MA: The MIT Press, 1965; *Language and Mind.* New York: Harcourt, Brace, Jovanovich, 1972.

16. Cf. *Five Architects*, pp. 15-37; Eisenman, Peter. "House VI." *Progressive Architecture*, June, 1977, pp. 57-67; Eisenman, Peter. "Post-Functionalism." *Oppositions* 6, 1976.

17. Eisenman, Peter. *House X.* New York: Rizzoli International Publications, 1982.

18. Gandelsonas, Mario. "From Structure to Subject: The Formation of an Architectural Language." In: *House X,* op. cit., pp. 7-31.

19. Libeskind, Daniel. "Stars at High Noon." in Hejduk, John. *The Mask of Medusa. Works 1947-1983.* New York: Rizzoli International Publications, 1985, pp. 9-22, p. 16.

20. The masque projects are documented in *The Masque of Medusa,* op. cit.

21. For a discussion of the history of masques, see: Strong, Sir Roy. *Art and Power: Renaissance Festivals, 1450-1650.* Berkeley: University of California Press, 1984.

22. Specific reference is made in this project to the American Midwest of the 20s. Hejduk. *The Mask of Medusa*, p. 428

23. Libeskind. *Stars at High Noon*, p. 16.

24. El Lissitzky, quoted in: Zygas, Kestutis Paul. *Form Follows Form. Source Imagery of Constructivist Architecture, 1917-1925.* Ann Arbor: UMI Research Press, 1951, p. 63.

25. Haag Bletter, Rosemarie et. al. *The Architecture of Frank Gehry.* Minneapolis: The Walker Art Center, 1986.

26. Jacobs, Mary Jane. *Gordon Matta-Clark: A Retrospective.* Chicago: The Museum of Contemporary Art, 1983.

THE SOURCES AND SORCERERS OF SUBVERSION

Within this clearing, the project of the modern continues. Over the last two decades, a number of architects have been exploring the possibilities of using modernism's urge to reduce architecture to a functional, abstract representation of a technological society as an act of revelation rather than as one of style. Projecting a modern world itself can be an act of criticism. This belief is extremely romantic, insofar as it asserts architecture's critical abilities to change society. In this act of rediscovery at least five different strains coexist. *Revelatory Modernists* continue the optimistic utopianism of modernism, but in a fragmented or deformed way, seeking to uncover existing processes of modernization rather than posing new ones. The second group, *makers of "shards and sharks,"* affirm modernization as a purposeful violation of certainty, blowing up or undermining buildings and leaving only fragments. These "shards" can easily become "sharks," strange beasts invading the comfortable social, economic, and physical status quo. Such enigmas cannot be consumed, and will remain always "other," undefinable and subversive. A third group takes the formal elements of architecture and feeds them back on themselves. These *textualists* take the linguistic analogy to its furthest extremes, deconstructing the texts by which and in which we live. The *new mythologists* use narrative qualities of language, often appropriating techniques derived from psychotherapy, modern literature and cinema, to construct alternative worlds. Lastly, the *technomorphists* appropriate most of these techniques, seeking to remake them into artifacts, extensions of the self as machines. They seek to remake both the self and the world in order to fulfill the project of the modern.

Many of these strategies were first articulated in the teaching, designs, and publications of several schools, most notably the Architectural Association in London and the Institute for Architecture and Urban Studies in New York. The Architectural Association was founded in 1846 as a private organization for the advancement of architecture. By the middle of the next century, the Association had become centered around a school, although it maintains an active social and publications program. In fact, its ability to exist as an experimental laboratory for architecture is due as much to its bookstore, bar, restaurant, publications and exhibitions, as to the actual teaching conducted in the school. Moreover, its expensive private program attracts students and teachers from all around the world. For the last fifty years the Association has fulfilled an oppositional role, offering alternatives to the status quo. During the 1950s, this opposition was directed at the humanization of modernism in the design of public projects. At this time the Association developed its reputation for the production of large-scale, rather hard-edge, and visionary projects. These visions combined a fascination with the purely technological with an interest in the organic aspects of technology, viewing structural systems, circulation, and the process of construction itself as an animate being requiring a biomorphic expression.[1]

This biomechanical tendency finally climaxed in the explosion of Archigram, a group of visionary designers first established in 1964. The members of Archigram, including Peter Cook, Ron Herron, and others, extrapolated from technology outside of the realm of architecture, proposing cities based on living capsules, wandering around the world, floating in the ocean, taking over cities, and plug-

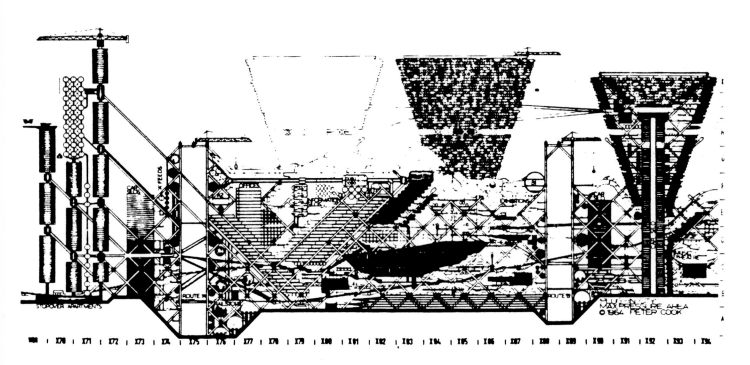

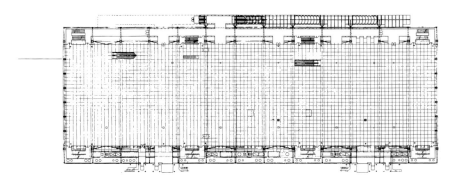

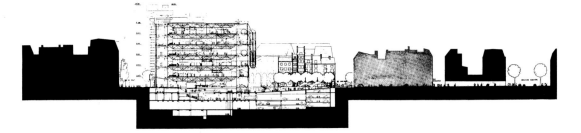

ging into highly developed support systems wherever convenient. Adapting images of Pop Art, Archigram's utopian schemes were presented as advertisements, necessary outgrowths of the development of our culture, rather than as the imposition of a purely technological utopia. This biomechanical architecture would free each individual by atomizing those structures housing the necessities for everyday life, making them infinitely available and adaptable.[2] The social would be constituted by the communal services allowing for this disbursement. But Archigram ignored the essential process of production, preferring to see the world as inhabited solely by a series of isolated consumers.[3]

By the 1970s, the influence of the Archigram group had created the most vital *high-tech* group in the world. Spurred by engineers such as Ron Herron and Ove Arup, and influenced by such early technological expressionists as James Stirling, young architects began proposing that mechanical and structural systems comprising our buildings do not need cladding, restricted functions, or even an immediate relation to any context. The great victory of this group came in 1972, when Richard Rogers and Renzo Piano won the commission for the Centre Pompidou in an international competition. Their scheme fulfilled Archigram's dreams, from the individualized viewing of art to the incorporation of billboard technology. However, what was actually built combined an enlarged modernist freespan interior with an exteriorized structure and mechanical systems. As a fulfillment of the modernist dream, it stands encased in the very suppressed elements enabling its conversion to reality. The mechanical and constructional components took over, becoming both the physical reality and the architecturally composed representation of the building, while the freespan and adaptable world opened up by those services became completely enclosed.

RICHARD ROGERS
PARTNERSHIP
**PA Technology Laboratories
and Corporate Facilities**
Princeton, New Jersey, 1984
Photo: Otto Baitz

In the following decade, Rogers, Piano, and Norman Foster led a group of mainly British architects who turned to an absolute veneration of structure and mechanical systems, producing buildings as intricate and expressive machines. In the Hong Kong Bank by Foster, 1985, or the Lloyd's of London by Rogers, 1987, all of the care taken in the production of a machine was finally applied to the scale of a building. The result was a pair of gleaming set pieces, alien beings of highly polished metals, extractions and celebrations of the inner logic of the surrounding buildings. The Lloyd's building, even at a modest height, is one of the purest skyscrapers ever built. Its exposed elevators, mechanical systems, and structure soar unencumbered by either skin or slab. The placement of the vertical circulation elements fills out the idiosyncrasy of the site, allowing a pure volume to rise in the liberated

center. The whole building is severed from the ground, allowing the city to flow underneath, and is tentatively anchored to the site with seemingly retractable tentacles. Renzo Piano applied his interest in building systems to the fringes of architecture – designing cars, sailboats, and feats of structural bravura – although he became more well-known for his ability to use conventional cladding systems to integrate architectural technology with a given context.

By the mid 1970s, the high-tech style had developed into the production of very sophisticated

showpieces of a technology that, upon exposure to the exterior of the wall usually hiding it, was styled and composed into something else. Demonstrating Archigram's dreams of infinite flexibility, these buildings, to the degree they were imposed upon the site, also expressed alienation. Although defined in terms of a forward reaching technology, upon their construction the manufactured palaces of commerce – banks, computer firms, car companies, and even residences – were already empty representations of a future now past, fixed in space, and stabilizing their set of working relations.[4]

Archigram theorist Peter Cook continued to teach at the Association, his work tending towards the biomorphic and away from the ever-slicker mechanical world of the high-tech architects. Architects such as Leon Krier brought a distinctly reac-

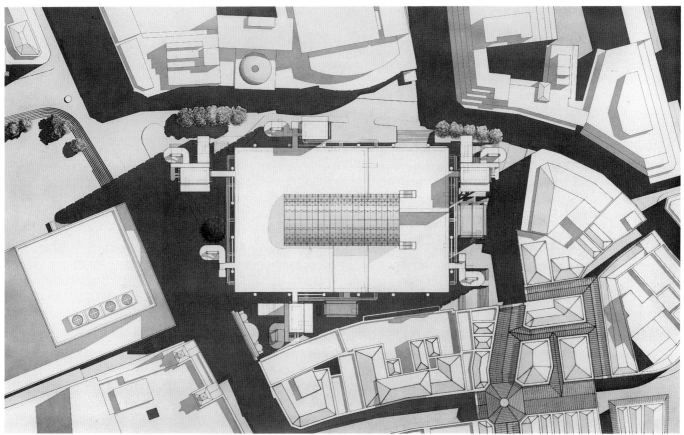

OFFICE
OF METROPOLITAN
ARCHITECTURE
City of the Captive Globe
1978

tionary tendency to the school; but other units of the program allowed newcomers such as Bernard Tschumi and Rem Koolhaas to develop their theories. Both architects were interested in the narrative aspects of architecture and in the reconstitution of the city through fragmented experience.[5] Both were disinterested in expressing technology for its own sake, and did not see the machine as an organic and alien being. They rediscovered the machine in the reductive, mechanized, and streamlined forms of modernism of the 1920s throughout the 1950s. Sharing a special interest in modernism's contamination by reality, they championed forms that had been fragmented by use or by integration in the urban environment, or that had been contaminated by impulses to monumentalize or vernacularize revelations of the new. Seeking the intersection between the liberation of the new and its transformation of daily life, they investigated how modernism worked. Their teaching coincided with the rediscovery of the most radical work produced in the aftermath of the Russian revolution. The work of Chernikov, for instance, became a historically validated antidote to high tech, all the more compelling due to its unrealizable nature.

Both Tschumi and Koolhaas continued their research at the Institute for Architecture and Urban Studies in New York. Founded in 1970 as a New York base for several out-of-town institutions, and as a research laboratory for urban theory, the Institute, under the direction of Peter Eisenman, became the American equivalent of the Association. An active publication and exhibition program sustained a lively debate, which ended in 1983 when Eisenman left his position as director. The Institute also maintained an extremely conservative strand, serving as the conduit into America for the the rationalist schools of Milan, Venice, Ticino, and Buenos Aires, yet allowed Tschumi and Koolhaas, as well as English theoreticians Kenneth Frampton and Anthony Vidler, to fully develop their ideas. *Oppositions*, the Institute's journal, introduced alternatives to conventional architectural history and theory to American architects, while exhibits focused attention on late modernist work in Japan, and on constructivists such as Ivan Leonidov. Tschumi produced *Manhattan Transcripts*, a piece of architecture in the form of a series of collages, structured as movie murder mysteries. Koolhaas researched and wrote *Delirious New York*, a book first exposing the chaotic and vital reality of New

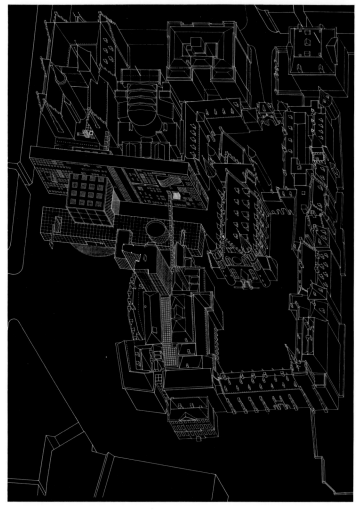

York by analytically stripping away the ordered facades exiling this activity from previous architectural debates, then proposing a series of myths, visions, and buildings to develop this vitality. Eisenman's theoretical research, the romantic modernism of Koolhaas and Tschumi, and the rationalism of the Hispanic contingent, set the stage for an exploration of alternatives to traditional ways of making architecture.

More than anything else, the A.A. and the I.A.U.S. validated the investigation of architectural issues as a form of criticism. They developed an integration of historical research with architectural form, a visionary projection of architectural possibilities, and an analytical deconstruction of existing reality – proposing oppositional architectural strategies.[6] Four figures investigated these issues so extensively that they became gurus of late modernism: Rem Koolhaas, Bernard Tschumi, Daniel Libeskind, and James Wines.

Of these four, Koolhaas most clearly continues the tradition of modernism, while his work was also the first to be widely copied and disseminated. Koolhaas first came to attention after winning the 1978 competition for the Houses of Parliament addition in The Hague. With confident bravura, he slashed through centuries of additions surrounding the Dutch "sacred precinct" of the Binnenhof with slabs skewered by round towers and gridded, tilted planes. Although not awarded the commission, he was given the job of renovating the Koepelgevangenis of Arnhem in 1979, one of several 19th century Benthamite prisons in Holland. His design mirrors Michel Foucault's archaeological investigation into the origins of order in Western civilization, proposing a renovation that both reinforces the prison's rationalist form and imposes a constructivist cross, one of whose arms escapes from the enclosing circle of the prison. With these two projects, Koolhaas set the tone for his architectural investigation. On a heroic scale, he fragmented modern architecture's formal devices, intersecting the ground plane, its urban context, and the

OFFICE
OF METROPOLITAN
ARCHITECTURE
exploded axonometric
**Renovation
of the Koepelgevangenis Prison
Project**
Arnhem, The Netherlands, 1980

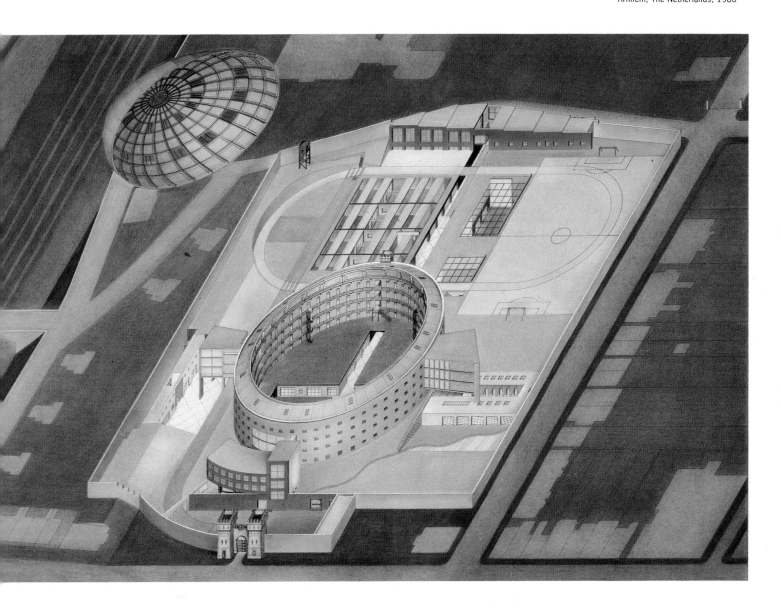

OFFICE
OF METROPOLITAN
ARCHITECTURE
perspective
**Project for the Renovation
of the Bijlmermeer District**
Amsterdam, The Netherlands,
1987

buildable – without becoming part of them. The dream of perfect, machined, and ordered functional elements only exists in Koolhaas' work as refractions that break through the surface, or as potentially dangerous fragments of the physical status quo.

In the 1980s, Koolhaas moved his Office for Metropolitan Architecture to a row of buildings in Rotterdam's housing trading companies. The firm's name suggests that he is a builder of the modern metropolis whose perfect intersection of physical forms is produced by rational planning, according to the needs of a capitalist society. The abstraction of this process of planning is

transformed into visible images, seemingly irrational, but attesting to a usually concealed intentionality. Koolhaas expresses the noncommittal, abstract and large-scale design that has replaced Beaux-Arts planning as modern architecture's fundamental activity, while eliminating abstraction, accreted forms, and the justification of functionalism. A cosmological mapping replaces this justification, seeking to intersect the new construction with a projection of the temporal and spatial conditions comprising it. In a housing project in Amsterdam, parallel slabs are bisected by the diagonal of the pre-existing road; a bridge in Rotterdam is turned into a monu-

ment to the port and an entertainment center.

Much of the constructed work produced by the Office for Metropolitan Architecture tends to be dominated by nostalgia for a bygone era. Its tendency towards abstraction and pure revelation, and forms expressing a revolutionary violence, stand in for a resolved architecture made from the cones, arcs, and dynamic diagonals of constructivism, the underlining of the slab of the Dutch *nieuwe zakelijkheid*, and the biomorphic forms of the 1950s. At best, as in the proposal to retro-fit the Corbusian new town of Bijlmermeer outside of Amsterdam, or in the project for

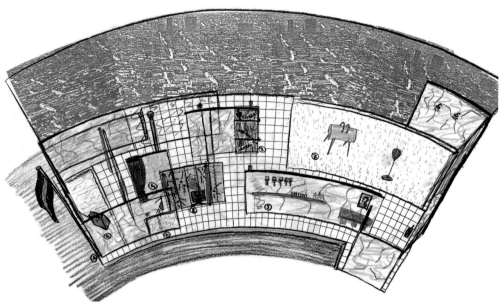

OFFICE
OF METROPOLITAN
ARCHITECTURE
plan
La Casa Palestra Project
for the Milan Triennale
Milan, Italy, 1986

Melun-Sénart, Koolhaas' work uses the forms as tools uncovering the topology – revealing how man orders that landscape, and proposing man's ultimate liberation through necessarily incomplete projections, whose function is to create voids, enigmas, and contradictions.[7] Recently, the Office for Metropolitan Architecture has produced more romantic works which decompose architectural elements. Their proposed Sports Museum, 1989, made out of chainlink fence cages, reduces the building to only a suggestion of rational enclosure. A series of villas takes the Villa Savoye one step further, allowing ramps to activate space conceived of as disconnected planes, walls, and columns. Architecture vanishes into a series of gestures. The connection between this disappearance and the human body is made overt in a revision of the Barcelona Pavilion as a weight room: modernism stands revealed as a kind of back-to-nature nudism. On a larger scale, they tilted up the section of a hill, underneath which the new train *grande vitesse* will pass in the industrial city of Lille, revealing this new machine's beauty. The heroism of this gesture, and the ganglia of bridges and tunnels it creates, express communication's role in the reestablishment of this former industrial center.[8] The evanescent and abstract nature of a communication-based society is revealed and fixed by a natural ridge of office buildings, forming the landscape of this new drama of modernization.

Koolhaas' significance seems to lie in the influence of his images, whether in the work of students such as Zaha Hadid (see Chapter 5), or in the work of a new school of "romantic modernists." The most prominent of these is the firm Arquitectonica, whose work exudes a love for materials of modernism (gridded marble, metal-and-glass curtain wall assemblies), combined with an expressive urge unburdened by morality. Such surrealistic compositions challenge the notion that buildings are only functional and respond to the need for architecture as advertisement. They have already shown that modernism, when carried to a logical extreme, can market the modern as a desirable consumer universe, removing architecture from the established structure of society, and situating it within the process of consumption. As an expression of a lifestyle, architecture can become part of the world of advertising. Thus the fragmentation of the modern, and its romantic belief that it can continually transform the physical environment, has become a style which masks, rather than reveals, the underlying social and economic structures at hand. Deconstructivism has become this year's model for the architectural selling of the self as part of a continually changing society.

Bernard Tschumi has established a position of authority as the architect of the Parc de la Villette, the largest urban park built during this century, and as the Dean of the School of Architecture of Columbia University. Once a teacher at the Architectural Association (Koolhaas was one of his students), his career seems to have been directed towards eliminating the notion of architecture as a functional delimitation of space. For Tschumi, architecture is a form of social therapy. "To really appreciate architecture you may even need to commit a murder," he wrote in his "Advertisements for Architecture," 1976.[9] "Architecture is defined by the actions it witnesses as much as by the enclosure of its walls." To make architecture is to describe an action in an inventive and productive manner. That activity was, especially during the years Tschumi taught at the Association and at the Institute, a narrative one whose medium was words, photographs and drawings. He grafted fragments of a vaguely familiar architecture, or sometimes of a recognizable building or plan, onto another – thus evoking the whole and all of its social and historical associations without becoming burdened by its order. He also collaged images of bodies in specific settings – evoking action yet avoiding the conventional "closed narrative." These collages of grafts were composed into a series of drawings using filmmaking's storyboard technique of plotting out a sequence of shots.[10] His work directly refers to cinematic conventions – decomposing the city in

To really appreciate architecture you may even need to commit a murder.

Architecture is defined by the actions it witnesses as much as by the enclosure of its walls. Murder in the Street differs from Murder in the Cathedral in the same way as love in the street differs from the Street of Love. Radically.

order to recompose it in a completely mechanized fashion, an artificial world whose order has an internal logic. Central to its operation is a certain madness, violence, or even mystery,[11] which is explored in the culmination of his short project of the 1970s, the 1982 *Manhattan Transcripts*.[12] In this volume, a murder in Central Park and a chase

BERNARD TSCHUMI
axonometrics of Follies (above),
perspectives of Follies
and central area (below)
Parc de la Villette
Paris, France, 1983

down 42nd Street replace social amelioration, professional perfection, or internal consistency as the motive of the architectural product. In this manner, states Tschumi, he "transcribes an architectural interpretation of reality…so that the conventional components of architecture are broken down and rebuilt along different axes."[13]

In his design for the Parc de la Villette, Tschumi applies his working method to "real" buildings, also replacing the vague sense of death motivating an otherwise miasmic metropolis with one based on a reading of the architecture's historical place in our society. According to Tschumi, his design is the architectural equivalent of the psychoanalytic transference, a process in which a patient's fears surface on their "construction" of the therapist, enabling them to acknowledge and come to terms with their phobias.[14] Tschumi postulates that the whole modern city is sick, suffering from a mania produced by its pursuit of rationalism and technology to such an extreme that these goals become their opposite: madness and an organizational dysfunction – as enacted by the Parc de la Villette.

The park is organized by a grid of red pavilions. These nine-cube constructions are the most basic building blocks of childhood, geometry, a new architecture. The pavilions are also twentieth-century equivalents of the tollhouses Ledoux designed for Paris at the end of the eighteenth century. Marking the boundaries of the city, these tollhouses were the most succinct statements of the Academy's newly codified architectural order, both symbolizing and manifesting state authority. As such, they can be read as generators of modern architecture, and also as harbingers of a revolution making them irrelevant, while continuing the rationalizing processes which caused their appearance. Tschumi's pavilions of red grids are also codifications of

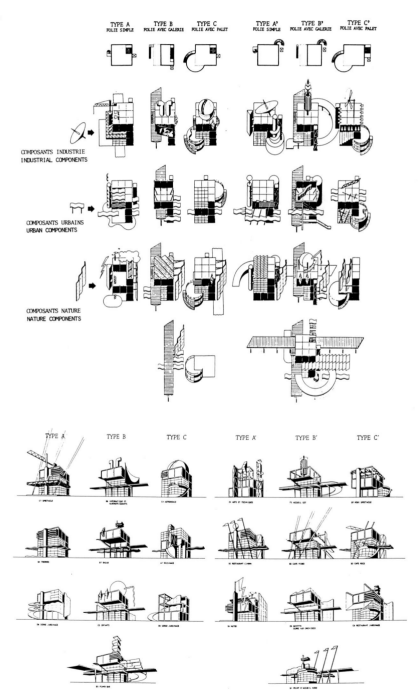

modern architecture nostalgically recalling the propaganda pavilions of the Russian revolution – perhaps in the hope that they will also engender revolution. Red, signifying danger, they are named follies – purposefully non-functional, a built craziness, the antithesis of order. **Architecture as revolution.**

Promenades cinématique, partially covered walkways replacing the boulevard, intersect these pavilions. A system for ordering and viewing the city, they cut through the layers of everyday logic, exposing the city to rationalization. The pavilions are covered with suspended, undulating roofs supported by a steel construction – mechanized ver-

sions of the portico, where architecture is reduced to its essentials and mediates between built order and its antithesis, nature.[15] The promenades are purposefully irrational, going nowhere fast. They replace the discipline of a column with the expressiveness of the machine, pushing architecture into its form of madness. This process continues in landscape projects Tschumi has turned over to other architects, rejecting the identification of gardens as natural equivalents of built order. In one sunken area, diagonals rhythmically break up the serenity of a Japanese-style gravelled area. Sewage pipes running overhead reveal the inherent logic of humanity's violence to earth's seemingly closed surface.[16]

The Parc de la Villette is the most complete statement of an architecture of violated perfection ever constructed. The park is a model for the anti-city, the city dedicated to creating differences, to defeating static enclosures of space and functionalism. It exhibits the power of architecture searching for a violent transformation of self, the necessary outcome of the pursuit of modernization. It reduces the architect to the role of "the originator of a set of combinations and permutations that is possible among different categories of analysis." Tschumi is currently utilizing this methodology in such projects

BERNARD TSCHUMI
simultaneous perspective
**New National Theater for Japan
Competition Project**
Tokyo, Japan, 1986

as the New National Theater in Tokyo or the reconstruction of Flushing Meadows in New York, which seek to "deconstruct architecture and opera" by denying the usual functional separations made for such cultural monuments, favoring "programmatic strips" and non-specific spaces. But in these more recent projects forms appear as part of a pre-existing language presenting traditional problems in a formulaic coat of revolutionary architecture.[17] Only in the statement of a non-building, a park, has Tschumi achieved the creation of a deconstructed architecture.[18]

DANIEL LIBESKIND
The Burrow Laws
1979

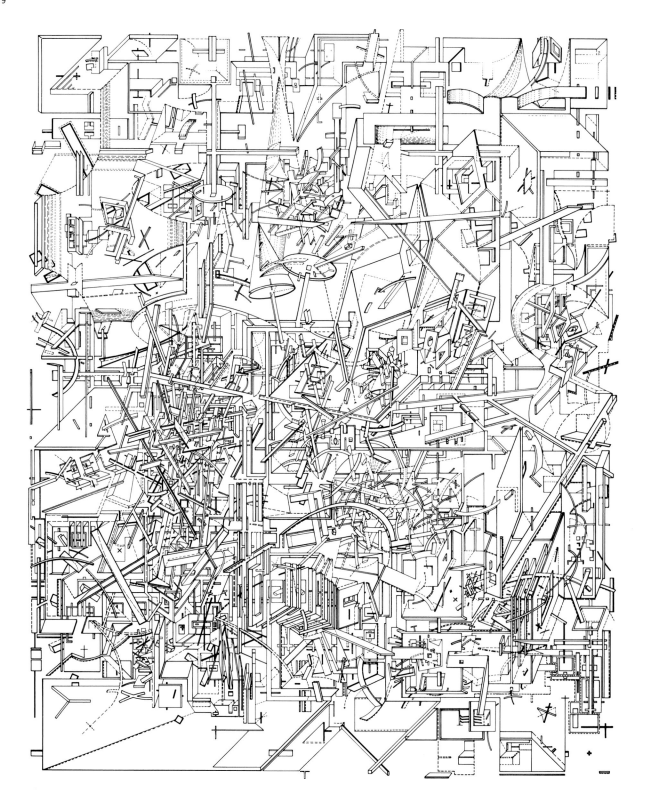

DANIEL LIBESKIND
Reading Architecture = Reading Machine
in
Three Lessons of Architecture;
Palmanova Project, Venice Biennale
Venice, Italy, 1985
Photo: Hélène Binet

Just recently Daniel Libeskind has begun to construct according to a working method he developed almost two decades ago. Trained at the Cooper Union under John Hejduk, his early work displayed a tendency to use fragmented abstract planes similar in style to Hejduk's. His work has become progressively denser and more abstract, while Hejduk has moved towards the creation of a three-dimensional mythology. Libeskind's collages of seemingly meaningless forms have further evolved into mere lines and strokes, an expressionistic version of the work of Cy Twombly. According to Libeskind, these drawings call attention to the fact that "Disorder, the arbitrary, born from the delirium of order pushed beyond its limits, by a strange paradox, discovers its own logic, a structure which, like an inaccessible and secret truth, has been prefigured in the alluring depth of chaos."[19] The architect's role is neither to impose order nor to oppose it with "mute monuments." Instead he can opt for an architecture that is "analytic, interpretive, symbolic, non-representational," and non-figural – "significance never fully exhausts its resources because there is always a residue left over which points to the correspondence or analogy that mediates the density of things and the ambiguity of meaning." Because there is no end result, only the "search for objectives," architecture is now considered "an act of research represented by a dense collection of data, whose validation cannot be found, but must be sought."[20] One must first accept the world as text, lacking any reality outside its legibility within the structure of signs. Libeskind then digs in, layers over, and grafts, rewriting these texts of the world (codes of nature, city streets, or literal texts) – not to make sense out of them, but to allow us to engage in an act of poetics which creatively explores the textual world. He exposes illegible texts either hidden in language itself or layered over by cultural production. More than the discovery of chaos, architecture becomes a direct engagement in the non-sensible world through the medium of drawing.

Libeskind and his followers are known for their concentration on drawings representing the world's density, whose architecture surfaces and rewrites its hidden texts. Inherently hermetic, Libeskind's methodology produces enigmatic maps of worlds, offering possible constructs ungraspable by our senses. They rupture our known world, and suggest another possible construct, uninhabitable, but inviting us to explore and alter it in response.

DANIEL LIBESKIND
Remembering Architecture =
Memory Machine
in
Three Lessons of Architecture;
Palmanova Project, Venice Biennale
Venice, Italy, 1985
Photo: Hélène Binet

DANIEL LIBESKIND
Writing Architecture = Writing
Machine
in
Three Lessons of Architecture;
Palmanova Project, Venice Biennale
Venice, Italy, 1985
Photo: Hélène Binet

His recent works more explicitly describe the maker as both explorer and transcriber, emphasizing craft. They also clarify his notion of an architecture articulating a transcendent world. An elaborate machine, constructed for the Venice Biennale of 1985, describes Western civilization's series of attempts to structure our world. A "reading machine," eternally rotating, offers a fleeting glimpse of a text, and represents the activity of a monk transcribing a received text. Camillo's *Theater of Memory* was the basis of a "memory machine," staging and projecting an alternative world. A "writing machine" demonstrates industrial society's maniacal condensation and recrafting of the world through a productive technology that in the end is merely self-justifying. In this last machine, Libeskind's architectural project becomes evident as an "unstable" and continually changing structuring of fragments: texts, maps, and mechanisms combine allusions and cosmologies in the image of technology. The machine produced has neither function, scale, nor a stable composition. Nonsense and obsessiveness function, as in the La Villette project, both as the real realm of the architect and as the liberating revelation of an accepted and closed system of reality.[21] Together they form the *theatrum mundi*, a theater of a new world inherent in ours, requiring an architect's performance.

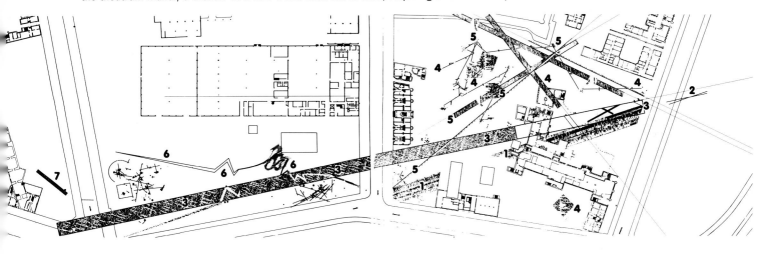

DANIEL LIBESKIND
plan
City Edge Competition Project
Berlin, Germany, 1987

Influenced by phenomenology, Libeskind now claims that his projects are "conceived with the specific meaning of metaphorical and indeterminate construction – architecture – and its capacity to reveal the truth of dwelling."[22] Romantically longing for a world beyond Western civilization, they seem eschatological. Libeskind describes the end of our culture as an opening up of possibilities rather than as the termination or fulfillment of modernization. Art and architecture have the potential to favor imagination instead of the given world. Once this world is over, and dreams are liberated, "architecture can stand violently outside of time."[23] His housing project for Berlin announces this new world by combining one of the axes of a new Berlin that Albert Speer, the ultimate architect as rational planner, hoped to impose on the city with a trace of modernist Mies van der Rohe's office. A model's textual covering lists the names of those who may have disappeared in the "final solution." Underneath this skin Libeskind buried his tools and prized books, and with them his very identity. An unstable block, lifted out of the ground, gestures to the sky and defies gravity, liberating these traces, these architectural endings.[24]

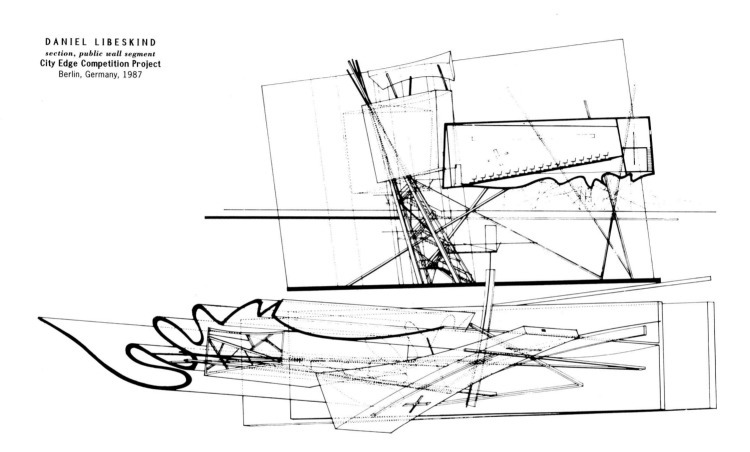

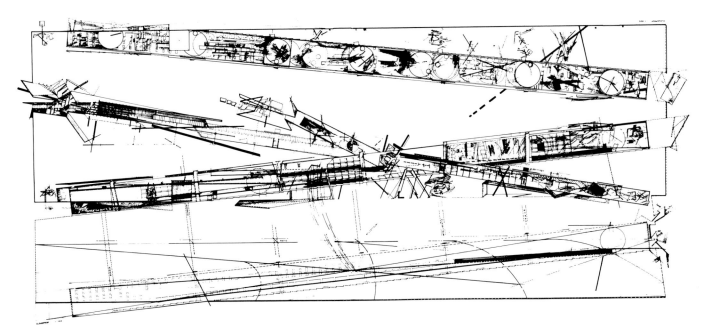

DANIEL LIBESKIND
Cloudprop
City Edge Competition Project
Berlin, Germany, 1987

Daniel Libeskind's architecture reads as a transcript of dreams comprised of memories, which for Libeskind can be both private and public, and are also able to project into the future. The continuum of an imagined and crafted world, where neither the self nor the other exist, a dream offers a potent antidote to the world of production and consumption, of isolation and alienation. The problem becomes one of uncovering dreams, and to this Libeskind responds with an obsessive reiteration of memory and projection, to the point that the surface of the page, or the skin of the building, disappears. Architecture, through this obsessiveness, continually transgresses the surface of the world as a sensible coherent system of belief. This can only be enacted by the maker and is incommunicable. The activity of architecture becomes an atomized analogy of personal liberation, offering alternatives to an architecture of social imprisonment through its reiteration of established values.

Against the romantic modernism of Koolhaas, the therapeutic narratives of Tschumi, and the obsessive liberation of Libeskind, James Wines posits a sculptural, concrete, and highly communicative alternative. Wines was trained as a sculptor, not an architect, and the name of his firm, Sculpture in the Environment (SITE), reflects its roots in late-1960s and early-1970s environmental art. To Wines, all art-making is essentially an activity of communication through the manipulation of the landscape, whether man-made or natural, a manipulation that primarily uncovers and remains open ended. Wines and his colleagues hope to allow the "sociological and psychological content" of architecture to escape from its formal constraints.[25] In order to free this "content," the formal composition of architecture must first be violated. Very few of the buildings SITE has produced in the past few decades take space, function, or construction for granted as building blocks of a logical structure.

SITE
Indeterminate Facade Showroom
Houston, Texas, 1975

Their work consists entirely of destabilizing the groundplane or the enclosing wall of a building which, if it isn't pre-existing, is constructed according to methods so standardized that they do not require an architect's expertise.

The major body of SITE's work has been constructed in the suburban shopping mall, the epitome of absence in American architecture. Their first project, the Indeterminate Facade, for the Best Showroom in Houston, Texas, 1975, heroizes this landscape, erecting an excessively tall and crumbling brick facade, seemingly left over from another civilization. The Notch and Tilt Projects of 1976 convert the blank boxes of a catalog company into billboards, advertising what Wines considers to be the inherent instability of our culture. This instability is literally covered up and diffused throughout the expanses of the suburban mall, a "managable functionalism." The Best Anti-Sign project in 1979 culminates this "signing strategy," after which SITE

began pulling pieces of the box apart, inserting vegetation, or placing petrified emblems of merchandise inside a "ghosted" double facade.

The whole notion of facade as a communicative face to a building, allowing the constructional assemblage behind to also function communicatively, was thus inverted. Wines then began to realize that the facade, even as an art project, continued to distinguish and sell the products of the company. Subsequent projects sought to bury the stores altogether. SITE became fascinated with the concept of the suburban mall invaded by the natural landscape it had replaced.

The decomposition of the facade culminated in the Highrise of Homes project of 1981. Wines proposed revealing the constructional and economic grid underlying the city and then allotting each owner a portion of that grid, still in its exposed state, to "cover" as desired.[26] The architect, as author imposing his own ideology and forms on the site, disappeared. Appearances, often the false faces of architecture, were abstracted into structure on the one hand, and then fragmented into a multitude of individualized contingent statements.

Having proposed methods refuting notions of architecture as a closed object, a servant to processes of production and consumption, Wines then decomposed the building's interiors. Walls remained as lath structure, semi-transparent scaffolding for whatever activities required definition. They refused any sense of closure, either for the rooms they surrounded, or for construction. Inhabitants, seen through their scrim-like structures, became actors in domestic dramas. Implements of daily life were petrified, surrealistic objects, everyday patterns broken up by sudden fissures.

By turning buildings into livable contradictions, open-ended and responsive, James Wines has pro-

HIGHRISE OF HOMES

SITE
Highrise of Homes Project
1981

posed the most fully realized deconstructions of architecture. Refusing to impose a single order, Wines acts as a magician whose wand transforms the everyday into a strange and indeterminate experience. "De-architecture," according to Wines, "is a way of dissecting, shattering, dissolving, inverting, and transforming certain fixed prejudices about buildings, in the interest of discovering revelations among the fragments."[27] Yet what is to be discovered, or why, remains unclear. As an activity, "accepting the disorderly nature of the universe and communicating this acceptance in his buildings" becomes the only content.[28] Because Wines works intuitively at carving away preconceptions concerning architecture and the world, his work never thoroughly critiques these orders. Wines would have us believe that social, economic, and physical determinants are so confusing and incomprehensible that they are chaotic. He refuses to apply his "de-archi-

tecture" to a constructive form of criticism that could assemble particular and related patterns of coherence, or systems of order, that contrast with the very monolithic and imposed orders against which he reacts. As a result he often ends up with closed objects which are one-liners, ambiguous and unfinished works that, as soon as they are posited in a physical and phenomenal setting with any clarity of order, become finished and comprehensible. His most effective work reveals these orders as a process. De-architecture's technique of communication is disengaged from the need for any constructive analysis.

1. The Association publishes extensive reviews of their student work every year, a practice that was initiated by Director Alvin Boyarsky with the publication of *Projects. Architectural Association 1946-1971*, ed. by James Gowan. London: The Architectural Association, 1972. The author is further indebted to Mr. Boyarsky for outlining a history of the Association during a conversation on April 21, 1989.

2. An interesting parallel might be drawn with the work of Richard Neutra, although his architecture is much closer to classic modernist lines. See: Marlin, William. *Nature Near: Late Essays of Richard Neutra*. New York: Capra Press, 1989.

3. Cook, Peter. *Archigram*. New York: Praeger Publishers, 1973; Banham, Reyner, "A Clip-on Architecture," *Design Quarterly* #63, 1965. The group, made up of Warren Chalk, Peter Cook, Dennis Crompton, David Greene, Ron Herron, and Michael Webb, got its name from their collective publication (architecture-telegram).

4. Cf. Davies, Colin. *High Tech Architecture*. New York: Rizzoli International Publications, 1988.

5. Tschumi, Bernard. "Spaces and Events," in Coates, Nigel (Ed.). *The Discourse of Events*. Themes 3. London: The Architectural Association, 1983, pp. 6-11.

6. Of course, this debate was not restricted to the Institute and the Association. Cooper Union, Columbia School of Architecture, the Yale School of Architecture, the Graduate School of Design at Harvard, the Cranbrook Academy outside Detroit, and numerous other schools formed a circuit of travel for architects and theoreticians, often for panels organized by the Institute. Schools became a meeting place for like-minded designers. In the late 1980s, the debate has become more diffuse, although schools such as the Southern California Institute of Architecture in Los Angeles, or the Stadelschule in Frankfurt, are attempting to recreate some of the intensity of debate that occurred at the Institute and the Association during the 1970s.

7. *OMA Projects 1978-1981*. London: The Architectural Association, 1981; "Office for Metropolitan Architecture." Special Section of *Archis*, March, 1989, pp. 12-51.

8. Donald van Dantzig, Project Architect. Conversation with author, April 19, 1989.

9. Tschumi, Bernard. "Manifesto 3. Advertisements for Architecture." Bernard Tschumi. *Architectural Manifestoes*. London: The Architectural Association, 1979.

10. Tschumi, Bernard. *Disjunctions*. Bernard Tschumi, *Luca Merlini. Neues National Theatre*. Tokyo 1986-1987. Berlin. Aedes Gallery, 1987.

11. Tschumi describes the manifesto as a contract to be violated and transgressed, linking his architecture with both the world of bureaucratic organization and its perversion in organized crime. *Architectural Manifestoes*, op.cit.

12. Tschumi, Bernard. *The Manhattan Transcripts*. London: Academy Editions/St. Martin's Press, 1982.

13. Ibid, p. 7.

14. Tschumi, Bernard. "The La Villette Park Competition." *Landscape. The Princeton Journal*, Volume 2, 1985, pp. 200-211, p. 207.

15. Cf. Vidler, Anthony. "The Scene of the Street; Transformations in Ideal and Reality, 1750-1871." Anderson, Stanford (Ed.) *On Streets*. Cambridge, MA: The MIT Press, 1978, pp. 29-111.

16. The sequence of gardens was designed by a team including Alexandre Chenetoff, Daniel Buren, and Jean-Louis Cohen. Cf. -- *Vaisseau de Pierres 2. Parc-Villette*. Paris. Champs Vallon, 1987, pp.64-72.

17. Tschumi "La Villette Park Competition," p. 207.

18. *Disjunctions*, op.cit.

19. Tschumi, Bernard. "Notes towards a Theory of Architectural Disjunction". *A+U* #216, September, 1988, pp. 13-15. This issue also contains an extensive review of recent Tschumi projects.

20. Libeskind, Daniel. *Between Zero and Infinity. Selected Projects in Architecture*. New York: Rizzoli International Publications, 1981, p. 27.

21. Ibid, p. 28.

22. Libeskind, Daniel. *Line of Fire*. Milan: Electa Spa, 1988.

23. Lecture by Daniel Libeskind at the Southern California Institute of Architecture, Santa Monica, California, January 18, 1989.

24. *Das Daniel Libeskind Projekt*. Berlin. IBA, 1987.

25. SITE. *SITE. Architecture as Art*. London: Academy Editions, 1980, p 6.

26. Wines, James. *Highrise of Homes*. New York: Rizzoli International Publications, 1984.

27. Wines, James. *De-Architecture*. New York: Rizzoli International Publications, 1987, p. 133.

28. Ibid, p. 134.

MECANOO
model
Groothandelsmarkt
Housing Project
The Hague, The Netherlands,
1988
Photo: Hans Werlempe

REVELATORY MODERNISTS

Within the family of four strategies architects are using to subvert architecture's role as the physical affirmation of the social, economic, and physical status quo, the *revelatory modernists* take the most conservative approach. Their buildings still intend use, are contextual, have a certain scale, and express an interest in perfecting modernism's abstracting and functionalizing tendencies. As mechanisms for improving the world, their subversive desires are channeled towards revealing the process of their own construction, as well as violating any complacent attitudes towards their perfection. Revelatory modernists reach beyond modernism to the degree that they uncover assumptions underlying a building, yet they also look back to its roots as a representation of our ever-changing relationships with the physical environment.

Much of this work is to be found in Holland, Germany, and France, where the connection between the formal properties of modernism, i.e. abstraction, functionalism, de-contextualization and liberation of constructional and spatial elements, has always been tied to social criticism. To young architects working in these countries today – and, to a certain extent, in America – the bureaucratic orders of the welfare state and the demands for a respect of tradition ameliorated by convenience have become deadening strictures replacing outright social repression. The question then becomes: How can these strictures be mined for their own transformation? The young Dutch firm Mecanoo has dedicated most of its career to this activity. While students at the architecture school of Delft Technical University, the five members of this firm won the competition for a block of social housing in Rotterdam (Kruisplein, 1985). The *plan libre* of the building did not act as empty space, but responded to complex housing and industrial regulations through flexible multileveled spaces expressing their technological apparatus. This "machine that fulfilled the promise of Le Corbusier"[1] also demonstrates Mecanoo's belief that a program should generate rather than determine

architecture, serving as a base from which to invent and add. Much of their work seems to refine the traditional Dutch housing block – an abstracted stack of isolated living units. But the interior has been purposely disturbed, transformed into an engine with working parts, while the exterior has

MECANOO
Kruisplein Apartment Building
Rotterdam, The Netherlands, 1985
Photo: Maarten Laupman

been broken, textured, and embedded with elements from the site that allude to its rebirth. This modernist and utopian dream envisions completely flexible living arrangements strewn across a new arcadia. Their own positions as the *poseurs* of such an order are confused by a proposed arcadia of fragments, and also by the camouflage paint covering their most assertive and imposing building forms.[2] In their project for the Groothandelsmarkt area outside of The Hague, 1989, they present a paradigm of modern society: social housing placed in a giant slab, severed from conventional notions of scale, context, and order – and also covered with camouflage paint. Endlessly repeating cells of private houses surround this "mothership." The block becomes a paradigm of communal living providing five social groupings, the cells a support system. Modernism disassembles itself, examining its parts while hiding behind the heroic mask of building.[3]

The firm of **Diener & Diener** uses similar forms. Their work is firmly rooted in the traditional white stucco forms of the Weissenhofsiedlung, which are layered with large-scale metal, colored stucco, or concrete elements. Their mixed use complex at Basel, 1985, divides the slab into individual pavilions, while the offices become an enigmatic supergrid. St. Alban-Tal Housing, 1985, uses site access and existing street patterns to deform its white block forms, as if the complex refines and comments on existing forms of housing. The interior courtyard becomes a private world of corrugated metal, culminating in a roof terrace lifted up to allow a view of the river and the city.

GÜNTER BEHNISCH
& PARTNERS
plan
**Central Library,
Catholic University at Eichstätt**
Eichstätt, Germany, 1987

The German firm of **Günter Behnish & Partners** manipulates modernism much more expressively. Interested in prefabrication and industrially produced building materials, the firm realized that a wholesale adoption of such methods allows architecture its "totalitarian tendencies."[4] However, that process could be inverted by breaking apart the prefabricated pieces, context, and program according to the problem at hand – resulting in collections of fragmented spaces and objects. Each one simultaneously expresses the potential perfection of mechanization and the multitude of chaotic human interactions permitted by a critical alteration of a typically closed system. In the Lorch Secondary School of 1982, the concrete structure is juxtaposed with a skin of glazing and metal. Each section of the school is a separate pavilion, its edges razor-sharp coverings – the tectonics reduced to abstract planes. In the middle a central courtyard rears up, providing space and light and pinwheeling the whole composition. This vortex of modernist instability aligns education with the enlightening power of the sun.

Behnish and Partners' high tech version of a rationalist, functionalist search for enlightenment and (chaotic) reason appears in other

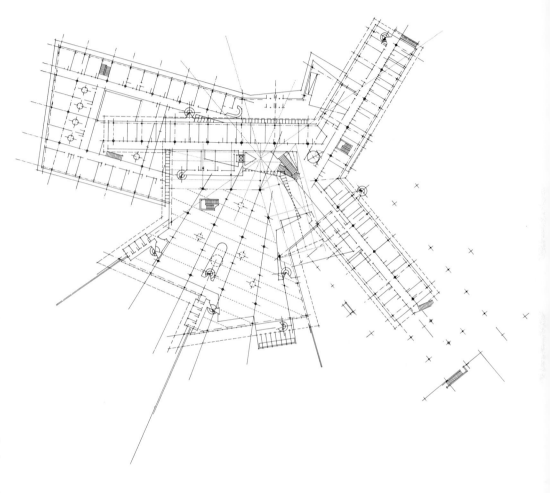

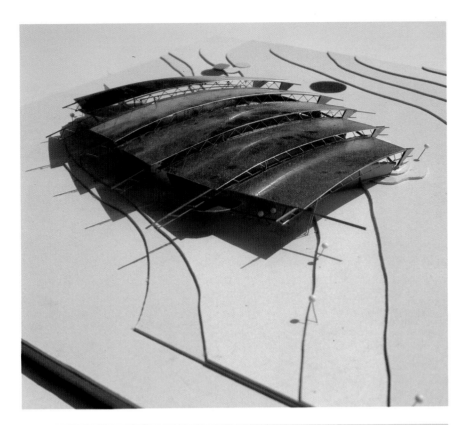

GÜNTER BEHNISH
& PARTNERS
models
Gymnasium Project
Bad Rappenau, Germany, 1989

institutional projects. Whole sections of buildings become deformed, breaking out of the box and tilting up from the ground plane. In the Library Building at the Catholic University of Eichstätt, 1987, walls lean and trusses elongate under the pressure of the explosive tendencies of the design. The enabling technology of the building – its glass skin, metal roof, concrete and steel structure – is stretched to the breaking point. Countless connections describe this tension. An interior or exterior view of the overall form of the building seems inherently unstable, and therefore unnotable. The building as a whole becomes its highly detailed parts: technology broken down to usable fragments, suspended in a delicate web of the memory of the former constraints of building. The work reaches its apotheosis in the Hysolar Building at the University of Stuttgart, 1987, where the structure's remains become a machine disclosing an invisible energy fueling the fragments as a group. Such a revelatory architecture requires no other justification.[5]

GÜNTER BEHNISCH
& PARTNERS
**Hysolar Institute Building,
University of Stuttgart**
Stuttgart, Germany, 1987

French architect **Jean Nouvel** has developed an architecture perfecting the "machine for living" and turning buildings into highly tooled machines. A series of bare cells makes up his housing project in Lille, 1987. Large scale openings, perforated metal skins, and a bullnosed end resemble a rationalist cage containing and revealing ever-changing daily activities. Nouvel's Institute du Monde Arabe is comprised of a wedge and a triangle incised by a diagonal. The building is thus split into two pieces, each the articulation of larger urban forces (the curving Seine on one side, the large Sorbonne complex on the other) that have co-existed without clarity for too many years. Inside, the spaces are further fragment-ed into balconies and loops of exhibition space. An inaccessible central, gridded courtyard, a memory of stable perfection, remains. Circulation becomes an internal machine, a celebrated construction of mechanized elements refusing clarity of space but allowing us to dwell on the process. The rear facade is constructed of a myriad of light-sensitive prisms, which, in accordance with optical and photographic principles, open and close according to the amount of available light. This continually working facade forms an unstable pattern, eternally recursive. Nouv-el's building emblemizes the modern – devoted to circulation, yet leaving spaces as undefined and floating planes. Enclosing within itself an unattain-able ideal, it also displays the ordered but interactive and changing nature of modernization.[6]

In the United States **Helmut Jahn** is undoubtedly the most successful manipulator of the technology of building. The main American representative of the English high-tech movement, he has produced a series of buildings demonstrating the extent to which the technology of constructing large office buildings and utilitarian structures can be used to reveal itself. The State of Illinois Center refuses to be a simple box, curving out into a smooth wedge escaping Chicago's deadening grid. A truncated conical form also rejects orthogonal order. Rising towards a skylight, its severed and unresolved lines imply the absence of a cupo-la typical of the civic building. Similarly, the requisite civic atrium, traditionally providing direct passage to the most important space in the building, leads only to bureaucratic offices, and thus has no function other than the exposition of the building. Its sides are covered with mirrors altering the relationship between individuals and the building into one that is inherently unstable, continually changing, destroying

HELMUT JAHN
State of Illinois Center
Chicago, Illinois, 1986

HELMUT JAHN
interior court
State of Illinois Center
Chicago, Illinois, 1986

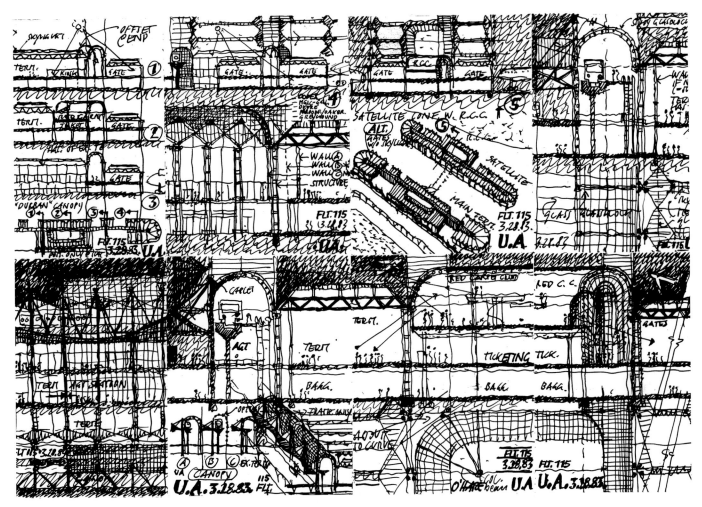

the intact gridded structure. Not even the center will hold, for there is a gap through the middle of the floor leading to the shopping arcade, exposing the usually hidden services allowing this building to function. Jahn extends this manipulation to elements such as the escalators – proudly displaying their mechanisms behind glass – yet adds on colonnades which reintegrate the building with the very community it undermines.[7]

In the United Airlines Terminal in Chicago, 1988, only air conditioning ducts, telephones, and lighting fixtures remain as emblems of order or as discontinuous monuments to the abstract systems of routine air travel. The structure of the building is reminiscent of the trusses of the great railroad stations of the nineteenth century. But these steel trusses are asymmetrical, suggesting both the terminals and the fuselage of an aircraft. Such romantic modernism is tempered by its antagonism towards any traditionally composed external form, or any distinction between ceiling and wall. Instead of a facade, this major public building has a continuous canopy on the interior or airport side, and a series of tubular sections on the tarmac side. The building is sliced into two parts which are connected underground by a tunnel. The United Airlines Terminal is the most radical decomposition of traditional architecture of any recent build-

HELMUT JAHN
sketches and interior
of concourse
United Airlines
Terminal 1 Complex,
O'Hare International Airport
Chicago, Illinois, 1988

RENZO PIANO
**Experiment of Reconstruction
in Otranto**
Bari, Italy, 1979

RENZO PIANO
sectional model
Kansai International Airport
Osaka, Japan, 1988

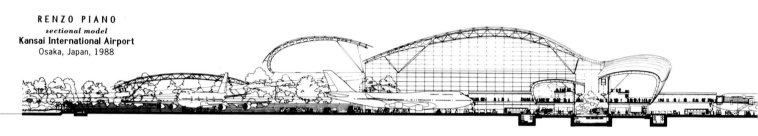

RENZO PIANO
detail
IBM Travelling Pavilion
1982-1984
Photo: G. Berengo Gardin

ing in America. Unfortunately its ready acceptance by the public and its use as an advertising tool suggest that the radical instability and unfinished nature of our society's systems is neither frightening nor liberating, but instead affirms the viability of those systems.[8]

Renzo Piano pushes high tech to the point where it almost completely disappears into engineering or nature. After ending his partnership with Richard Rogers, Piano concentrated on reducing the building's structure and skin to completely malleable elements in an open-ended system of construction, rather than designing boxes with externalized mechanical services. His 1984 greenhouse-like exhibition shed for IBM was an extrusion reducing architecture to the linear repetition of a single arc, a concept that he took to even greater lengths in a series of linear compositions culminating in the mile-long Kansai Airport project of 1989. He also designed enigmatic objects such as the Paris Bercy-Charenton Commercial Center of 1987, translating both a site created by the sweep of a freeway and the logic of spanning large forces into an object which directly expresses technology and science. In other projects the walls and spaces of his

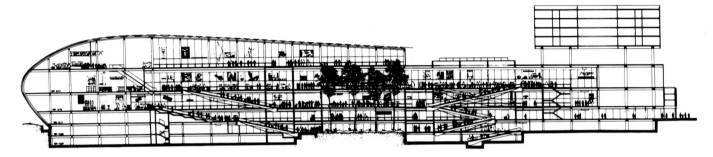

buildings attempt, as in the Menil Collection Museum in Houston, 1986, or in the Newport Harbor Museum of 1989, to disappear into their context. The working parts of the building – its doors, structural supports, and skylights – become the only identifiable elements of the construction. At its most abstract and grandiose, this architecture stretches steel and concrete to its very limits.[9] Resembling the work of **Santiago Calatrava**, whose tensile bridges and winged doors dissolve buildings into the incomprehensible flows of dynamic engineering, it furthers modernist architecture's tendency to represent the most current scientific thoughts.[10]

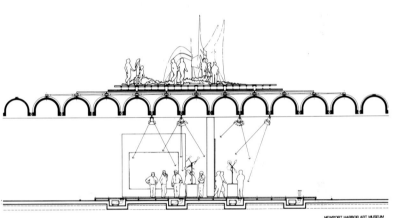

NEWPORT HARBOR ART MUSEUM
TYPICAL SECTION

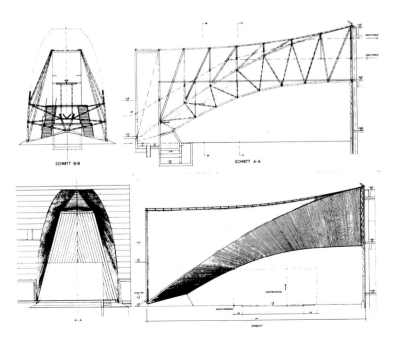

SCHNITT B-B

SCHNITT A-A

A - A

ANSICHT

Emilio Ambasz also extends the borders of architecture, exploring ephemerality and transience. His work concerns itself with making an environment more responsive to the body, and thus inherently changing. Designing everything from calculators, signs, and a highly successful line of chairs to building complexes, he blurs edges, uses abstract materials, and cuts through imposed systems of order with ergonomic and sensory perception-based design. In his projects for the Banque Lambèrt, 1985, and his New York Financial Guarantee Insurance Company Offices, 1986, scrims and lighting finally replace solid architecture altogether.

Such a disappearance can take a monumental form. An office building project in Mexico – a leaning slab of offices combined with a pool of water and windmills – harnesses the environment and makes habitation possible. The visible forms are enigmatic elements of a giant geometry marooned in the landscape. Ambasz is especially known for his buried buildings whose cut-off geometrical shards of glass protrude from the ground. The largest completed project of this kind is the Lucille Halsell Conservatory in San Antonio, Texas, 1988. There is virtual-

ly no building here, only curving ramps, expanding space and the undulating ground. Glimpses of structure disappear behind vegetation and seemingly arbitrary skylights, providing the non-architecture below with visibility. Ambasz shares an affinity with the work of SITE – burying buildings, leaving traces instead of monuments. In his latest projects, such as the proposal for the Nichii Obihiro Department Store in Obihiro, Japan, the building becomes a crystalline modernist mound containing only vegetation. Nature is here captured and made possible by an architecture of self-denial.[11]

DIANE LEWIS
detail, "Mae West"
Artist's Loft
New York, New York, 1989

MICHAEL KALIL
Project for Armstrong
World Industries
Interior Design Center
Lancaster, Pennsylvania, 1987
Photo: Langdon Clay

Michael Kalil, a designer who has worked with NASA, pushes abstraction even further. His environments are almost wholly composed of light and electronically-defined scrims, with heat sensitive control mechanisms that respond to the body. The environment he proposed for NASA is a communications center;[12] it is an architecture that promises the complete dematerialization of physical reality, favoring literal projections that are infinitely variable and completely intangible.[13]

Revelatory modernism logically leads to ever greater abstraction, but it can also tend toward its reversal – the disappearance of traditional architecture into the particular, the implemental nature of the vernacular. A group of young designers incises small machines into a larger context, creating a working model of modernity feeding on its overwhelming context. **Diane Lewis'** furniture activates blank space: a movable library subdividing a cleaned-out loft, a lawyer's desk whose movable parts animate the reception area's incised oval, or carved doors sliding the length of a loft. These doors are also art works mounted on tracks that can become scaffolding for whatever activities take place in the loft. Studs and electrical conduits become a decorative language highlighted by elaborate door handles. Such arts and crafts attitude empties its own context, except for the Empire State Building seen through a small hole cut in one

DIANE LEWIS
detail, suspended law cabinet
Law Offices
New York, New York, 1988

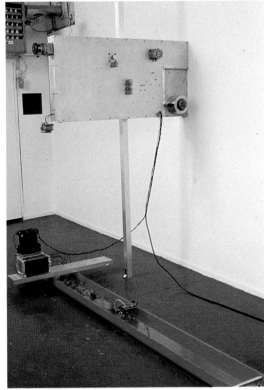

KEN KAPLAN,
TED KRUEGER
Bureau-Dicto Project
Dural/Ductile Project *(right)*
1989

of the walls. The work of New York designers **Kaplan and Krueger**, such as their Lamp-Table or Workstation, are similar in attitude: fili-greed objects motor their way through an abstract environment, changing from a vertical splayed lamp to an ironing board-like table. Incisions in the wall, crafted points of contact with a world disappearing into nothingness, have their own autonomy.[14] These are not just objects, however: in the imagina-tion of the architects, they are "Renegade Cities," mythical versions of our consumer society living out its most condensed desires and violent urges on a scale that is completely dependent on the atti-tude and interpretation of the viewer. Constructed of engine parts, pieces of metal and cast-off mate-rial, they present fragments of the future of our own vernacular.

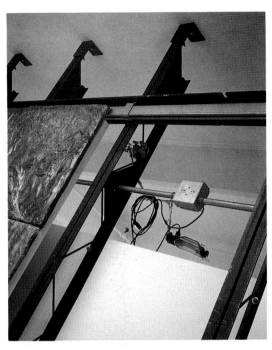

Architectural activity of this kind inevitably moves closer towards revealing the unknown. Steven Holl's walls, floors, and ceilings are incised with inventive gestures alluding to another world. He uncovers, digs into, and splays his walls, floors and ceilings – incising them with a story, one that perhaps invents a world more compelling than the one present in the actual room. The Fifth Avenue Apartment, 1983, and the Pace Showroom, 1986, both

STEVEN HOLL
planetary frieze
Guardian Safe Depository
Fair Lawn, New Jersey, 1983

use raw concrete with windows of heavily framed glass. The complex forces shaping these urban interiors stand revealed. Beams, columns, duct spaces and windows are all set off center and collaged in accordance with the inner necessity of the building. The void of this powerfully-reduced space focuses on the dramatic, ever-changing play of light. Layered incisions in the carpeting and glass suggest fragments of a geometry floating through space. As they recede towards the past, these traces of our lives' complexities project us toward a new world.[15]

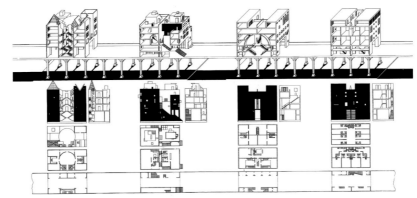

STEVEN HOLL
sections, plans
Bridge of Houses Project
New York, New York, 1981

Craft-oriented architecture suggests new worlds without building them, and considers architecture the pure making of artifacts organizing everyday activities. Such work implies a passive context, a world as *tabula rasa*, an audience awaiting organization. An imposed order, even if it is an incised one, is still sought. Yet Holl's urge to decompose the world around him into a series of isolated moments of coherence moves a step further. Before building, he researched the dog-trot house, the row house, and the other mostly functional reductions of architectural space produced in the American vernacular.[16] This interest in the vernacular is also expressed in such projects as the Bridge of Houses proposal for the unused, elevated train track in Manhattan, produced in 1981. Here, Holl as archaeologist first discovered an unused ground plane which he reconceptualized as a connecter slicing through the morass of New York, and a series of building elements with which to order the newfound land. The linearity of the site, created by the logic of mechanization, is layered with simple boxes and rooms, bare minimal gestures of architecture, and shot through with emblems of optimistic modernism, skylights, and glass-enclosed stairs.[17]

At times these investigations become a sculptural exploration of the massivity of walls, nostalgically seeking an absent certainty in modern building methods. But at its best, this kind of architecture realizes that the American vernacular is an engine of modernization, as worthy of exploration as any steel-and-stucco factory housing block of the 1920s. After all, Thomas Jefferson's simple block became an isolation cell, generating methods for transforming the landscape at the University of Virginia. Held together by a dream of an architectural and political coherence, it exists as a collection of independent and mutually cooperative elements. Jefferson's own house layered onto this investigation a fascination with the house as a kit of parts, a collection of movable walls, double-functioning objects and fragmentary functional elements.[18] Such interest in the malleable house extended to mass production and the development of the balloon frame.

The resurrection of the American vernacular house as an engine of modernization has become the half-archaeological, half-utopian task of a number of architects influenced by **Frank Gehry** in Southern California. Gehry was the first to strip away the covering of the balloon frame, destabilizing its interiors, and turning the making of architecture into an act of collage. Collage and assemblage, two thoroughly modern ways of making art, present the house as intrinsically incomplete, a microcosm of all the worlds out of which its materials and images are drawn. They are also an intrinsic part of the tradition of making homes in the new land of America, built of fragments of technology. The destruction of tradition requires any optimistic statement of its possibilities to become archaeological. Such a liberation must first attack and reassemble an already existing technology through reduction, abstraction, functionalism, and technological expressiveness. Although their work is by no means technological in appearance, many artists influenced by Gehry are concerned with manipulating technology in the manner of the reductivist architects of the 1920s and 1930s. Others realize that the working technology of our society is not quite so clean and streamlined, and design buildings that expose the invisible orders of our society, using the materials through which technology is expressed.

ERIC MOSS
plan
**3964 Ince Boulevard Building
Renovation**
Culver City, California, 1989

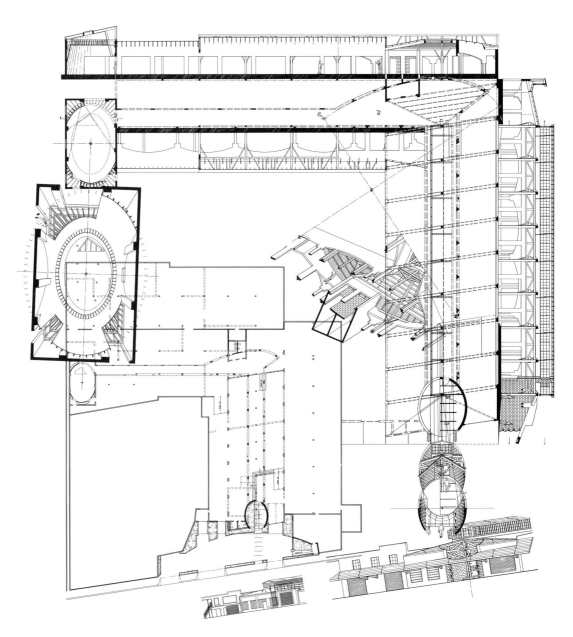

ERIC MOSS
interiors
**3964 Ince Boulevard Building
Renovation**
Culver City, California, 1989
Photo: Alex Vertikoff

The works of Eric Owen Moss, beginning with his Petal House of 1982, exemplify such activities. The walls, roofs, stairs, windows, and doors comprising the safe American home were pulled apart and recombined into ragged collages of discontinuous forms. Although his work was expressive, and, in the beginning, more akin to the communicative concerns of Venturi or SITE, his more recent work on a series of speculative office building conversions in Culver City, California, reveals an interest in actual methods of construction. The columns that stretch along the front and hold up the major space of the Ince Boulevard Building, for instance, are made of sewage pipes – invisible, mass-produced elements that enable buildings to work more than any structural member. These quasi-heroic elements stand in contrast to the tortured asphalt shingle roof forms, torn apart to allow light in and give scale to the building. Reinforcing bars form security screens or handrails. Throughout the building that which is hidden is revealed, put together with the inventiveness of a tinkerer rather than with the passion of formalism. Grand moments of architectural bravura do appear in the revealing of a pre-existing promenade of wooden columns and trusses, or in the carving out of a negative space in the existing context – an oval courtyard or a board room. These formless buildings, functional spaces carved out of a confusing context, reveal the underlying confusion around us.

ROB WELLINGTON QUIGLEY
Linda Vista Library
Linda Vista, California, 1988

ROB WELLINGTON QUIGLEY
exterior and garden (right)
House in Del Mar
Del Mar, California, 1986

In the Del Mar House of 1984, Rob Wellington Quigley assembled pieces of old craftsmen bunga-lows, California beach shacks, and renovated garages to create a village of isolated areas of activity flow-ing together according to patterns of use, lifted into the air. The garage, service, and private areas below became a concrete, gravel, and shingle "other world," a Zen garden-like retreat. Quigley created an intro-verted response, opened up in the underpinnings of cast-off architecture, washed ashore on the beaches of a Californian consumerist heaven.

ROB WELLINGTON
QUIGLEY
interior
Linda Vista Library
Linda Vista, California, 1988

Quigley's most accomplished work, the Linda Vista Library of 1987, stretches bowstring truss-es to open a shed bursting at its seams. A collage of materials from the confused suburban envi-ronment creates an amorphous box escaping its shopping mall site, mining the materials that built the community in order to describe it. The outside is a closed mission, a fortress of cul-ture staking its claim in the park-ing lot. The inside is a liberated world of articulated structure, lighting fixtures, and stacks of the most basic materials avail-able: wood, concrete block, and off-the-shelf furnishings.

CHRIS BURDEN
Samson
Henry Art Gallery
University of Washington
Seattle, Washington, 1985
Photo: Chris Eden

MC2
exploded axonometric
House Project
1989

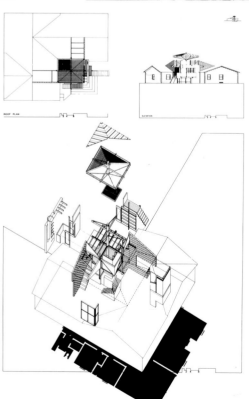

The New York and Texas firm MC2 pushes this revelation of the modernist reality of the vernacular to the foreground, constructing houses that are nothing but unstable layers of cladding tied together with a tentacular structure that fabricates a very livable house. Such assemblage structures are becoming more common in the American landscape. Only the most thorough collages go beyond mere collecting, to be formed into handles onto the invisible systems that allow their construction. But in America and Europe one can still not find the clarity of cutting and activating that exists in the realm of sculpture. The violent lesson of Chris Burden's battering ram *Samson* is a piece of wood applying increasing pressure on the room in which it is placed as more people view it, illustrating the self-destructive nature of all human making and consuming.[19] Above all, Gordon Matta-Clark proposed the pure act of cutting away, revealing elements that do not comprise our society, such as stubs of wooden studs or the broken planes of an office building's metal-and-glass assembly, rather than building an alternative. To him, building the act of cutting and discovery is a process integral to knowing the world by living out its contradictory orders.

1. Conversation with author, April 19, 1989.

2. Architektengroep Mecanoo. "Groothandelsmarkt, Den Haag,'s-Graven-hage." Report to the City of The Hague, Autumn, 1988.

3. Cusveller, Sjoerd (Ed.), *Mecanoo. Vijfen-twintig Werken*. Rotterdam: Uitgeverij 010, 1987.

4. Kandzia, Christian (Ed.), *Architekten Behnish & Partner. Arbeiten aus den Jahren 1952-1957*. Stuttgart: Ed. Cantz, 1987, p.6.

5. Cf. *Kandzia*, op. cit.

6. Pisanio, M. "Body Building: Today's Archi-tecture in an Impasse between Modernism and Post-Modernism." *Artforum* 20, April, 1988, pp. 102-106; Nouvel, Jean. "Impos-sible Urbanity." *Architectural Design* V. 50, #11/12, 1980, pp. 14-15.

7. Miller, Nory. *Helmut Jahn*. New York: Rizzoli International Publications, 1986

8. Paul Goldberger used Helmut Jahn's work to describe the extent to which architecture has become part of the culture industry. Goldberger, Paul. "Design: The Risks of Razzle-Dazzle." *The New York Times*, April 12, 1987, Section 2, pp. 1, 34.

9. Piano, Renzo. "Renzo Piano Building Workshop: 1964-1988." *Architecture and Urbanism*, March 1989.

10. Calatrava, Santiago. *The Daring Flight*. trans. by Savino d'Amico. New York: Rizzoli/Electa Publications, 1987.

11. Ambasz, Emilio. *The Poetics of the Pragmatic. Architecture, Exhibit, Industrial and Graphic Design*. New York: Rizzoli Inter-national Publications, 1988.

12. Russell, Beverly. "An American in Space." *Interiors*, May, 1984, pp.198-207.

13. Once again, the fine arts and cinema have pushed this potential much further than architecture has. Notable examples may be found in the work of Robert Wilson, especially in his designs for *Einstein on the Beach*, 1976, *Death Destruction and Detroit*, 1979, and *the CIVIL warS*, 1983. See: Wilson, Robert. *Robert Wilson. The heater of Images*. New York: Harper & Row Publishers, 1980.

14. "Kaplan, Krueger, Scholz." *Building Machines*. Ed. by Robert McCarter. New York: Princeton Architectural Press, 1987, pp. 28-41.

15. Holl, Steven. *Anchoring. Selected Pro-jects 1975-1988*. New York: Princeton Architectural Press, 1989.

16. Holl, Steven. *Rural & Urban House Types. Pamphlet Architecture 9*. New York: Pamphlet Architecture, 1982.

17. Holl, *Anchoring*, pp. 37-43.

18. Despite more recent works, this remains the standard description of Jeffer-son's inventiveness and his relation to American architecture in general: Kimball, Fiske. *Thomas Jefferson, Architect*. Boston: Houghton Mifflin Co.,1968 (1916).

19. Ayres, Anne (Ed.). *Chris Burden. A Twenty-Year Survey*. Newport, CA: New-port Harbor Art Museum, 1988, pp. 146-147. Burden exposes the violent underpin-nings of the urban environment more than any architect.

GORDON MATTA-CLARK
Conical Intersect, Beaubourg
Paris, France, 1975
Photo: Estate of Gordon Matta-Clark

SHARDS AND SHARKS

Using enigmatic, dangerous, and unknowable forms, the *makers of shards and sharks* play a treacherous game. Their program is to uncover, mimic, and deform processes of modernization by either using forms seeming to have a life of their own or ones indistinguishable from their chaotic context. These architects track down elements of modernization posing behind a mask of convention, display a pseudo-facade of composure, which they proceed to explode, and salvage fragments with which to rebuild. Although the forms produced may resemble those of revelatory modernists, there is less concern for the revelation of structure and the transformational potential of their architecture. Instead, the makers of shards and sharks share a subversive impulse to plant a bomb under existing social and economic structures as represented in building, creating the act rather than its consequences. Most deny that their work presents a social critique, either describing their activity on formal grounds or seeing their work as an expression of intensely personal and intuitive urges. This work lurks in the depths of the modern city and consciousness, showing its sharp fin-like edges, an enigmatic and dangerous cut through the skin of stable society, or maybe only a reflection of our dangerous and violent times.

Designers on the edge of this extreme position construct radical forms unidentifiable as architecture, indistinguishable from the work of such sculptors as Richard Serra, Chris Burden, Robert Wilson or Walter Pichler, except for the intrinsic desire to confound notions of habitation and communication. Even this distinction is blurred in the work of **Tadashi Kawamata**. This Japanese artist invades homes, stores, and galleries with truckloads of wood slats. He creates curved forms that stretch through a building, confusing traditional uses and complicating its original form, much of which is covered up or made irreverent by the sculptor's intervention. Almost the whole facade of the Tetra House, 1983, is covered with wood. Passage into some rooms demands negotiating a "Merzbau" of wood. The wood echoes the planar covering and structure of the existing house, and, without revealing its structure, makes more of it.[1] Later projects such as the Nove de Julho Cacapava Project, constructed in Sao Paolo, 1988, take on a life of their own, swirling around like some of Gor-

TADASHI KAWAMATA
detail
Tetra House N3 W26
Sapporo, Japan, 1983

detail section
Way Out West: Berlin
Berlin, Germany, 1988

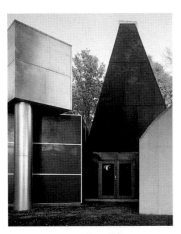

don Matta-Clark's later projects. Again, it is Frank Gehry who has most recently taken this development the furthest. Acknowledging Giorgio Morandi, Richard Serra, and Matta-Clark, Gehry created a series of enigmatic objects, most notably the 1987 Winton House in Wayzata, Minnesota. The inhabitation of this house is irrelevant to the celebrated juxtaposition of materials and forms, which do not quite unite in an overall composition, and whose powerful presence disturbs our sense of scale, function, and logical comprehension. A long tradition of architects mine the tools and elements of their trade in order to uncover the dangerous implications of their own activities. Peter Cook, one of the leaders of Archigram, and now in partnership with Christine Hawley, is godfather to them all. Cook and Hawley have taken the organic technology of Archigram and blown it up, leaving only fragments of structure and an underlying set of connections beneath walls of vegetation. The building remains as a collage of previous constructions, abstract grids or unfinished forms. The logical outcome of this preoccupation with our "new" unstable world is to build, because of or despite, its confusing and rich nature.[2]

A large and international group of young architects, many of them students, are pushing modernist abstraction to fragmentation, conjuring the dangerous forms of the city, and collaging its enigmas into tentative, yet menacing constructions. Journals are filled with drawings that respond to both the bomb planted by their saboteur teachers and the explosion's aftermath. Dimitri Vannas and Roland Cowan, two students at the Architectural Association in London, sum up some of these attitudes:

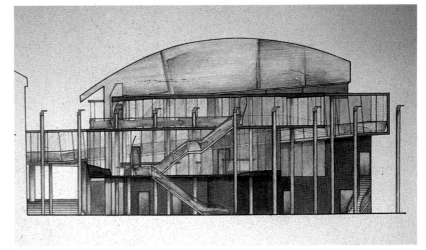

Everyday events are challenged by being given an extraordinary, unpredictable volume or location.... The initial, simplistic volume is progressively articulated, so that the materials which define it generate their own narrative, using the structural principles as ordering devices. Dimensional description is not appropriate here. Planes become articulated, and begin to acquire character.... Explosion as a strategy questions the established role of internal and external space, allowing the emergence of the ambiguous, transitional space in between.... The result is a kind of architectural composition in which the elements are personally interpreted and invented, obeying a *kinetic theory of architecture*.[3]

DAGMAR RICHTER
Berlin Fuhler/Berlin Topographie/
Berlin-Vernetzung Implosion
Project for
Berlin - Denkmall oder Denkmodell
Exhibition
Berlin, Germany, 1988

This architecture seeks continual motion, "unbuilding" as fast as society keeps building, desiring overwhelming confusion. Dagmar Richter's theoretical projects and competitions are layers of incomplete walls floating off of grids, cantilevered over a tilting ground plane. Tentacles reach out to anchor these elongated structures, but nothing orders the structure, enclosure, and gesture, which are intensified by the sheer complexity of her drawings. In Richter's 1988 theoretical project for Berlin, the ground lifts up to reveal a computer chip, suggesting a more revelatory intention. This work is gestural, not constructive, seeking an explosion followed by an exploration of the architectural qualities of its fragments.

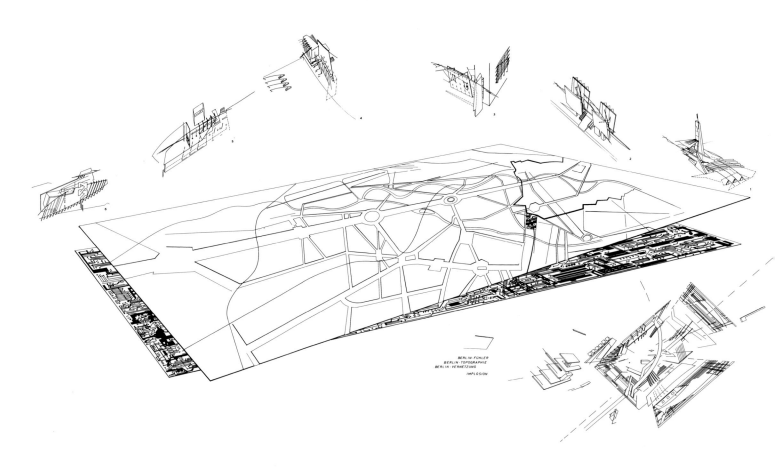

BERLIN-FÜHLER
BERLIN-TOPOGRAPHIE
BERLIN-VERNETZUNG
IMPLOSION

Austria seems an especially fertile breeding ground for such activities, producing both the so-called Graz School,[4] headed by Gunther Domenig, and the delicate irreverences of Coop Himmelblau in Vienna. These architects dedicate themselves to complicating and making more rococo the modernist tradition. Domenig's fairly conventional practice has evolved into an intuitive and expressive method. Previously obsessed with order and geometry, he now utilizes "the other aspect of geometry," the unknowable potential of all of its measurements, to find "the new architecture...behind the facade or in the earth."[5] The Stone House, 1989, "a place where expression and contents merge,"[6] exemplifies this. Although one can analyze the building as a series of enclosed bedroom forms grouped around a large open living room with a view to the lake and anchored to the ground by a long jetty, such a functional description inadequately explains the architecture. The house is a mess of angled walls, cut-off acute corners, metal roofs, and unexplainable protuberances. These elements form a mass of stone holding a crystalline form. The house

ADOLF KRISCHANITZ
interior
House in Salmannsdorf
Salmannsdorf, Austria, 1987
Photo: Margherita Krischanitz

becomes a built analogy for the ground from which it rises, allowing for a liberated experience within its battered walls. It is a molded mass that is infinitely articulated and then lashed together on the inside with highly crafted elements. Domenig describes the house with drawings of stone and vegetation that evoke both a spiral sensation of falling into the depth of the place, and an Icarus-like feeling of ascent. The house, to him, is his body, our bodies, and the whole earth. By refusing to make sense, by being a dense mass of material, it refutes the analytic splits we make between ourselves and the world.

Adolf Krischanitz's work is much quieter, almost rational. His exhibition pavilion in St. Pölten is a series of simple, primary shapes. But the round form is covered with a corrugated material, the yellow bar adjacent to it is cut through with a red cross, and blue planes curve across its sensible facade. Some of his work recalls an Adolf Loos on acid. His Salmannsdorf House is a barrel vaulted structure covered with a nervous pattern of brightly covered tile. The interior's decomposition of the Loosian abstracted and unstable interiors continues with the insertion of orange walls, the extension of ceiling planes with cantilevered metal lighting fixtures, and the insertion of round windows framing a stable view of the outside world. Lamps based on Rietveld's Three Tube Lamp, 1924, juxtapose brightly colored horizontal and vertical planes that recall De Stijl. The overall effect is purposefully too jarring to represent a prelude to its own disappearance.[7]

ADOLF KRISCHANITZ
exhibition pavilion
**Birth of a Capital City
Exhibition**
St. Pölten, Austria, 1988
Photo: Margherita Krischanitz

COOP HIMMELBLAU
conference room
Rooftop Remodelling
Vienna, Austria, 1989

The firm of **Coop Himmel-blau** is undoubtedly the most provocative of young Austrian architects. The early collaborative work of architects Wolf Prix and Helmut Swiczinsky is closely related to that of Archigram. They never lost their desire to undermine convention by the affirmation of its radical alternative. But now they build those alternatives while refusing to state their autonomous existence. "Architecture must burn," they proposed in 1980, calling for a design giving form to the contradictions and pace of the modern city, rather than retreating from that challenge:

We are tired of seeing Palladio and other historical masks.... We want architecture to have more. Architecture that bleeds, that exhausts, that whirls and even breaks. Architecture that lights up, that stings, that rips, and under stress, tears. Architecture should be cavernous, fiery, smooth, hard, angular, brutal, round, delicate, colorful, obscene, voluptuous, dreamy, alluring, repelling, wet, dry and throbbing.[8]

Having surveyed the profession, and burned part of it with their Burning Wing project of 1980, they claim that "architecture is dead."[9] What then is to be done? For Coop Himmelblau, the irreverent and idiosyncratic expression of the "energy fields" of our world remains. To uncover those fields, the walls, roofs, and stable relations to ground and gravity that give us a false sense of security must be ripped open and something else, something alien, must be inserted.

This alien can be characterized by openness: "open mind, open spaces," declares Prix. Spaces are indeterminate, as are enclosures. The two partners first make dense sketches – *"psychograms"* – representing what they want to achieve "without contingencies – zoning, how it stands up, laws." They then carefully translate these enigmatic and intuitive sketches into reality.[10] In the Lawyer's Office in Vienna, 1989, the corner of a nineteenth-century building becomes the landing pad for a strange beast. That beast, whose wing dangles dangerously over the cornice, has only one function: to house the conference room. The rest of the offices extend back in white spaces opened up in the former attic. The construction of the wing is made possible by a truss in tension, a stretched fabrication of steel anchored at the highest point. The myriad thin members of this truss, and of most of Coop Himmelblau's structures, diffuse loads to the point where they become competing poles of attraction instead of fixed points of reference. These thin members also make the underlying order of architecture transparent, leaving a series of overlapping planes, shimmering and sheer coverings that may be either ceiling or wall. Coop Himmelblau seeks to prove that freedom requires tearing down the monotonous walls of our social and physical prison house.

When building something new, as with the Funder Factory in St. Veit/Glan, 1988, Coop Himmelblau begins with the technical constraints that must be liberated. Why should a chimney not dance, they ask, turning industrial production into a chaotic

COOP HIMMELBLAU
Rooftop Remodelling
Vienna, Austria, 1989

COOP HIMMELBLAU
Funder Werk 3
St. Veit/Glan, Karnten, Austria,
1988

mess held together by shifting plates and taut cables. For the new town of Melun-Sénart, they proposed a street fight between "dense Manhattan" and "laid-back Vienna," to expose the potential of modernization's conflicts. Architecture here is a gestural act combining personal and social liberation. Their architecture calls to mind the power chords of 1960s rock and roll, which Prix is addict-ed to, a discordant and liberating slash at conventions, unrestricted by logic, and striking out for the sake of its own statement. In the work of such young architects as **Reinhardt Honold** and **Wolfgang Poschle**, this rebelliousness becomes more radical, and is expressed in tougher materials: their shards do not become wings, but bombed-out bunkers.[11]

England is another active center for the construction of shards and sharks, especially at the Architectural Association. The work of **William Alsop & John Lyall** can serve as an example. Some of their projects barrage the viewer with an eclectic mix of materials and forms, based on an interest in high tech and other forms of technological expressionism. Their mixed use project for Herouville-St. Clair in Nor-

mandy, designed in 1989 in association with Jean Nouvel, Otto Steidle and Massimiliano Fuksas, is composed of stacks of rectangular and tubular sections forming sleek office towers sectioned off, skewered on a thin core, and bisected by a dark metal mechanical slab. A curved metal shape housing a bridge and aviary is echoed in other projects. Most of their recent work mixes fragments of highly refined structural grids and sleek skins with gestural sweeps of steel and glass. This English high tech is marked by its frenetic extremes of overdetermination and complex idiosyncrasies, exploding as a result of its internal combustion.

Architectural Association teacher **Peter Wilson** currently works in Germany as well as in London, and is building the new Municipal Library in Muenster, West Ger-

many. Wilson's trademark is the "bridgebuilding," which exploits the beauty of construction technology's concern with connections and relations, and whose structure translates orthogonal forces into the active realm of triangularization. Wilson then layers a skin of fragments, overlapping planes, and extending frames over this technology, creating their narrative.[12] In the Library, the bridge provides a circulation element, the space in between

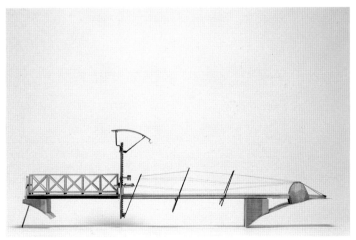

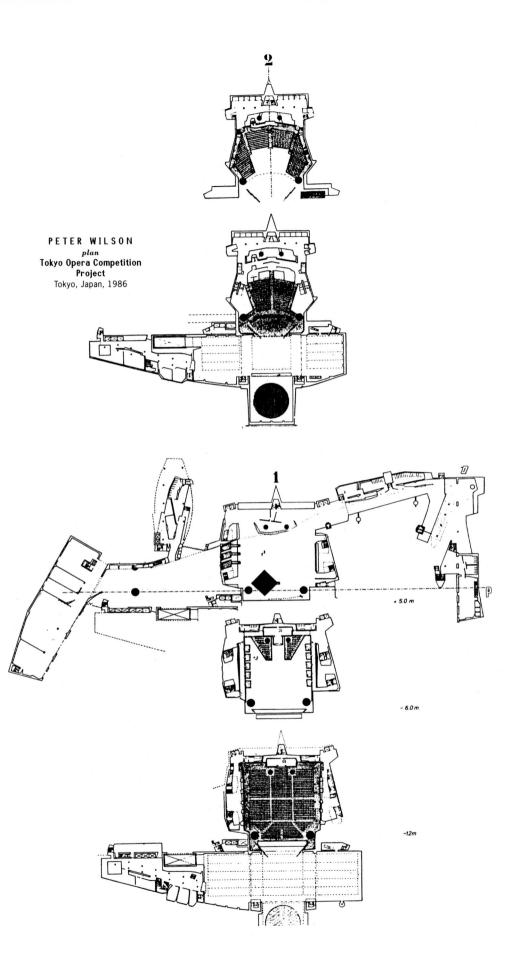

PETER WILSON
plan
**Tokyo Opera Competition
Project**
Tokyo, Japan, 1986

two shards, one curved, one combining splayed forms. The architecture here is coming undone and exposing public spaces below, although it still actively possesses the site. It is, says Wilson, "an active as well as representational mechanism of the city." In his project for the Tokyo Opera, this mechanism becomes more explicitly technomorphic – a large beast invading the city.

Dutch architect **Jo Coenen**'s earlier projects, especially his City Hall for Delft, 1986, and his pharmacy in Eindhoven of the same year, fragment modernism. In his designs for the National Architecture Museum, currently under construction in Rotterdam, he begins to re-examine the nature of architecture itself. There, an open, gridded box, the sanctuary of modern architecture, floats above a pool of water. Isolated in its grand perfection, sheltered by a classical colonnade and an expressive roof, it reminds us of architecture's origins in shelter and order. Red walled compounds surround this mirage of perfection; bridges shoot through the complex. Architecture has been taken apart and the pieces left dangling. This building turns a monument into a declaration of the inherently constructional, contextual, and unstable nature of architecture.

JO COENEN
Health Clinic and Pharmacy
Eindhoven, The Netherlands, 1987

JO COENEN
perspective
Dutch Architecture Museum
Rotterdam, The Netherlands, 1988

JANEK BIELSKI
model
**West Hollywood Civic Center
Competition**
West Hollywood, California, 1987

For America, as for revelatory modernists, the confused collection of materials and forms invented and utilized to make sense out of a land perceived as newly found provides a context. Janek Bielski, a native of Los Angeles trained at the Architectural Association, simultaneously expresses an interest in the explosion of high tech and a love for his land. His competition entry for the West Hollywood Civic Center of 1988 consists of a functional bar of offices distorted into a boomerang shape by the configuration of the roads. Its responsiveness to the curving sweep of the automobile-scaled street is increased by the

JANEK BIELSKI
model
Desert House Project
1989

skin of the front facade, a supergrid of steel and glass suspended like a billboard for modernity, and held away from the standard construction of the actual building. Behind, the council chamber is placed underground, a modern version of Pueblo and Anasazi Indian kivas. The courtyards are microcosms of California's various landscapes. Bielski continues his interest in the arid landscape with his Desert House of 1989, where the high tech structure of the house barely peeks above the ground, a world refusing to participate in the rape of the surrounding landscape.

WILLIAM ADAMS
model
Malibu House
Malibu, California, 1988

William Adams' collages reflect Venice, California's helter skelter environment, which is the testing ground for current fashions and drugs. His house and studio, designed in 1988, is made of layers of curved metal, blank stucco walls, and fragments of a steel and glass architecture. Overlooking a small courtyard oasis, it is defined by

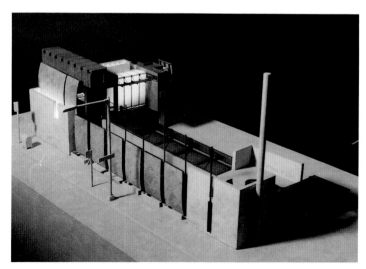

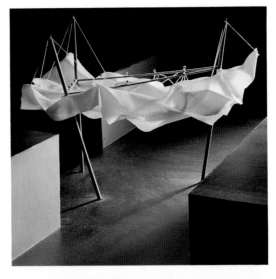

the surrounding tough urban forms. Visions Architects, based in San Diego, take the flotsam of the city and collage it onto grand arcs and fragmented grids, indicating, but never completing, an order. Their work resembles its suburban, atomized context rather than the more rarified and intact worlds of either order or nature. Tom Grondona revels in this less easily definable world. In a store in a San Diego shopping mall, completed in 1986, he uses the HVAC systems and structure to form a chaotic order. The stub ends of a rational order are vividly painted; additional gratuitous pieces of metal and stucco further confuse the senses.

Japan's fast-growing consumer culture engenders its own form of shards and sharks. Designers there delight in enigmas of uncertain scale, function, and material that disturb and threaten the status quo.

TOM GRONDONA
collage
Morgan's House of Furniture
San Diego, California, 1988

TOM GRONDONA
ceiling
Claudia's, Horton Plaza
San Diego, California, 1986

Biotechnic design – in Japan coming out of the metabolist tradition – posited the building as an intrinsically coherent organism, which the younger generation must now break away from. Kazuo Shinohara, the oldest of this generation, has expressed an abiding interest in the beautiful chaos of the modern city. He intuitively connects this beauty to a theory of chaotic and dissipative structures, buildings representing this state of flux, the "in between" of matter and our knowledge of matter.[13] Shinohara's boldest project, the Tokyo Institute of Technology Centennial Hall, lifts a tube, sliced down the middle, high above the street. This "machine in the air" hovers over planes of glass and steel, its inverted eye peering out like some monster turned on its belly, but ever on guard. Inside, the rooms underneath the tube are impacted by its low curve, creating a strange sense of incomplete shelter. Shinohara and other Japanese architects working in a similiar style have perfected an architecture refusing classification as building. Remaining a threatening potential solidified into bulging forms, its qualities of perfection and completion can only be discovered in between, or beyond, these buildings.[14]

Among younger architects such as Riken Yamamoto, Atsushi Kitagawara, or Hajime Yatsuka, this work becomes both lighter and more technological in character, but remains willfully strange.

122

KAZUO SHINOHARA
Tokyo Institute of Technology
Centennial Hall
Tokyo, Japan, 1987
Photo: Masao Arai/The Japan Architect

KAZUO SHINOHARA
interior underneath restaurant
Tokyo Institute of Technology
Centennial Hall
Tokyo, Japan, 1987
Photo: Masao Arai/The Japan Architect

According to Botand Bognar, "their art of fragmentation is an attempt to create non-forms and withhold meaning, or alternatively, cancel them before they can take shape and solidify into univalent and deterministic entities." This will constitute a new form of industrial landscape, he believes, as poignant and enigmatic as a *haiku*.[15] In **Hajime Yatsuka**'s Media Luna Building in Kobe, 1989, several office buildings – one of concrete, one of glass, and one of silvery metal – seem to have collided and become layered over each other. The building becomes

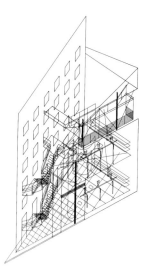

metaphoric for the accumulative nature of the modern city – a strange conglomeration of otherwise normal forms intersecting to create great arcs and sweeping curves. In the Angelo Tarlazzi Building in Tokyo, 1987, the collision is more filligreed, as if responding to the acute triangle of the site and the electrical lines around the building. The building is made up of brightly colored fragments of more solid constructions, held in place by cords in tension and grids seemingly as arbitrary and willfully mysterious as the forms themselves.[16] **Riken Yamamoto**'s Rotunda Building in Yokohama, 1987, an enigmatic void constructed of the various walls and construction grids making habitation possible, is an arched

screen lifted high above a terrace. **Itsuko Hasegawa**'s Shonandai Cultural Center, constructed in Fujisawa in 1989, miniaturizes the city into a mountain of huts bisected by a road suddenly becoming snake-like, culminating in a silver globe. Although the whole world can thus be captured by the obsessive intensity of the modern metropolis, its meaning remains enigmatic – out of scale, alien in its materials and beyond reach.[17]

RIKEN YAMAMOTO
Rotunda Building
Yokohama, Japan, 1987
Photo: Botand Bognar

Perhaps the most poignant and disturbing work is that produced by **Atsushi Kitagawara**. Kitagawara, like many other young Japanese, uses his designs to rework or deform the basic building blocks of the modern city, whether they be imported Western images, traditional Japanese elements or the skins

and futuristic imagery inherent in modern construction practices. While the Mesa Building, for instance, takes curtain wall construction to an extreme, the 395 Building warps Japanese concrete grid patterns both inside and out, as if their imprisoning structure can barely contain the bulging forms within. The Rise Building of 1986 is the most complex and evocative of Kitagawara's designs. It is a multi-use miniature of the frenetic city around it, covered by a lead shroud that has been partially pulled back to reveal the entertainment contained within. Its copper curve, truncated pyramids and floating screens map the confusion of the city onto a formerly stable architecture that now plays hide and seek with the stability of function, entrance, and structural

determinism. A series of cracks and fissures animate the building, allowing recognizable references to appear and disappear as if the architect were merely operating the curtains and backdrops of the city. Architecture is no longer merely a scaffolding, it is a complete stage set for a play about the city.[18]

Picking up the shards of this modernist explosion requires accepting the current state of both architecture and life, and believing that it

ATSUSHI KITAGAWARA
details
Rise Building
Tokyo, Japan, 1986

ENRIC MIRALLES
plan
Civic Center
Hostalets de Balenya, Spain, 1986

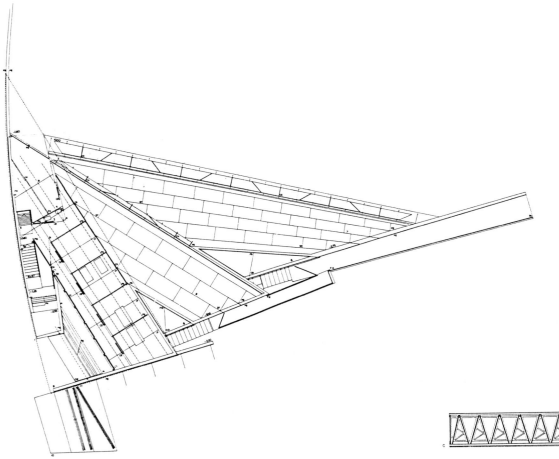

ALVARO SIZA
sections, elevations
**Faculty of Architecture
University of Porto**
Porto, Portugal, 1987

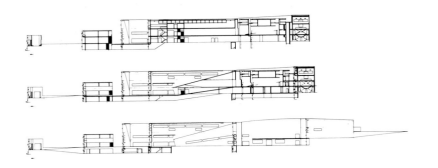

can have direction. A more elegant and subdued version of this process can be found in the work of **Arturo Silva** and **Enric Miralles**, who practice south of the Pyrenees. Their work is also much more calibrated. Major functional elements in Miralles' Social Center for Hostalets, 1989, are contained in the triangulated trusses, which make possible the sweeping roof covering its major open spaces. The whole center appears as a sharp fragment of an unimaginably large refinery whose explosion scarred the ground.[19] Silva's work is smoother and more subdued. He shares a fascination for triangular shapes, here defined by white walls. His few houses and a bank building in Oporto, Portugal, are composed of triangles and smooth curves independently moving past each other, allowing light to carve out a third order of shades and shadows. This elegant fragmentation opens to the orthogonal order of the city, allowing for a sense of liberation, although the actual spatial relationships of the buildings have only been remodeled.[20] In the hands of the firm of **Powell-Tuck, Connor and Orefelt**, this strategy can lead to the design of a modern-day palace, the Villa Zapu, Napa Valley, 1987. Here modernism is reduced to 1980s wit and pinpoint grace.[21]

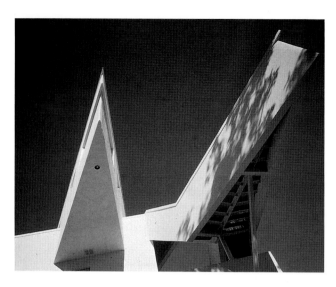

POWELL-TUCK,
CONNOR & ORENFELT
detail
Villa Zapu
Napa Valley, California, 1988
Photo: Richard Waite

POWELL-TUCK,
CONNOR & ORENFELT
Recording Studio Complex
The Power House Chiswick
London, England, 1987
Photo: Richard Davies

The Atlanta firm of **Scogin, Elam and Bray** pieces together elegant collages of shards. Their WQXI Radio Station project of 1987 combines the romanticism of broadcast technology with the sophisticated revision of a constructivist plan. Designing a small bridge for an office park, they hung a rock at the highest point of the delicate shape, turning the simple act of traversing a monotonous landscape into

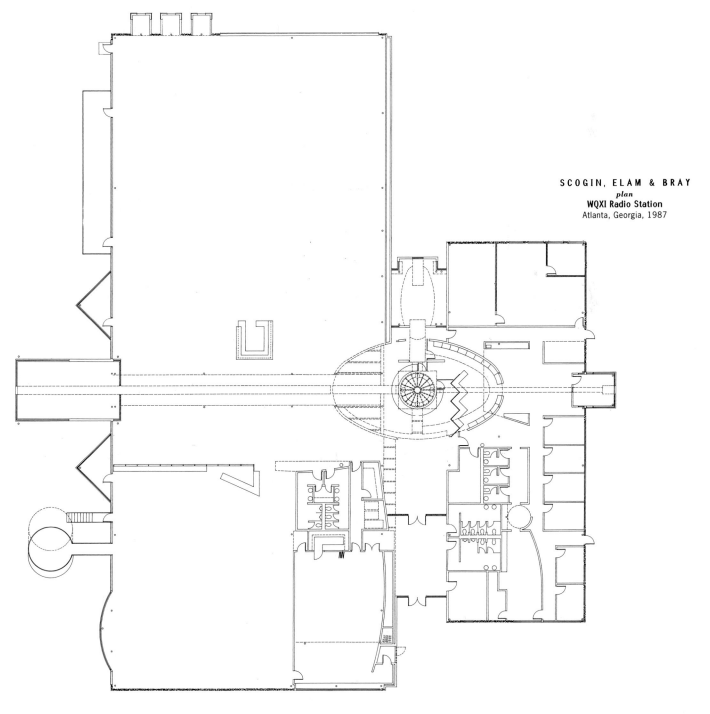

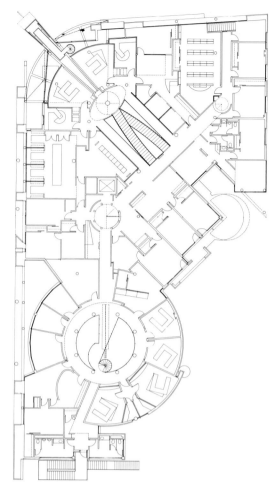

SCOGIN, ELAM & BRAY
plan
Headquarters Library
Clayton County Library System
Jonesboro, Georgia, 1988

an essay on connection and danger. Their vocabulary includes roofs rising to triangular gestures, metal bracing exposed and turned into aediculae. Each plan form and connection is articulated, overlapping and incomplete, creating a confusing collage in three dimensions. Their Clayton County Library of 1985 uses the cheapest building materials available (prefabricated steel trusses, "Butler building"-like metal assemblies and off-the-shelf furnishings) to create grand gestures: a seemingly industrial reading room, exterior nooks as attached pavilions, and a wall painted like the inside of a bookcover. Scogin, Elam and Bray hint at larger orders and grand statements that cannot be imposed on their suburban context.

SCOGIN, ELAM & BRAY
Headquarters Library
Clayton County Library System
Jonesboro, Georgia, 1988
Photo: Timothy Hursley

SCOGIN, ELAM & BRAY
interior
Headquarters Library
Clayton County Library System
Jonesboro, Georgia, 1988
Photo: Timothy Hursley

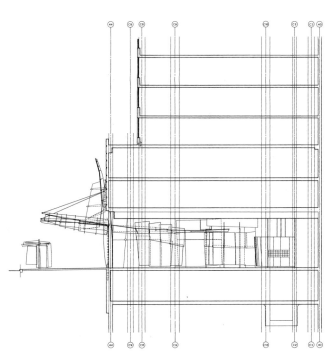

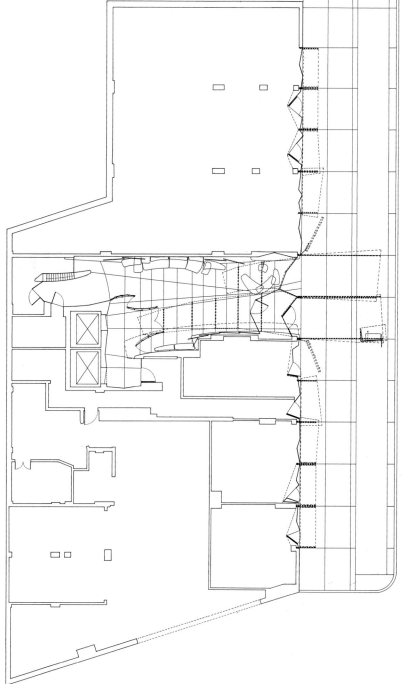

The work of the Chicago firm of **Himmel & Bonner** uses similar forms. Their renovation of the Playboy Enterprises office building of 1989 covers its walls with curved and sharp edges of an alien technology intruding into a controlled corporate environment. But only the forms are different: the commentary is purely formal and not tied to specific materials. The work of **Krueck & Olsen** more radically pursues form-making's disappearance into an explosion of fragmentary planes and lines, based on the steel and glass grids that identify the Chicago School's downtown home and its surroundings. Their mirrored shards

**CENTRAL OFFICE
OF ARCHITECTURE**
interior space collage
Wolff Residence
Los Angeles, California, 1989

create a combination of reflections, layered edges, and shifting ground planes – a nightmare of modernism – constructed of elegant and detailed materials that articulate one's expensive existence.

Projects produced by firms such as the **Central Office of Architecture** in Los Angeles exhibit the most theoretical version of this kind of work. Their proposal for downtown Los Angeles cuts away at the large scale and anonymity of its environment with cantilevered planes and diagonal chunks excised from its skin. They seek to reveal the hidden structure of the city, and to collage on to it the scaffolding the new and inherently unstable world that exists on the roofs, in skewed angles, or in left-over voids of the modern city.[22] Their "Recombinant Images in Los Angeles" proposes that viewing and making the city are unified.[23] Architecture builds the consciousness of this city of shards

**CENTRAL OFFICE
OF ARCHITECTURE**
perspectives
Urban Study: Object Zone
Los Angeles, California, 1989

and sharks, faintly remembered terror and absurd hope. Yet all of these architects deal resolutely with the modern world as a projection on a blank page, as an image. Their work concerns itself with creating an aesthetic, and set-designing the modern city.

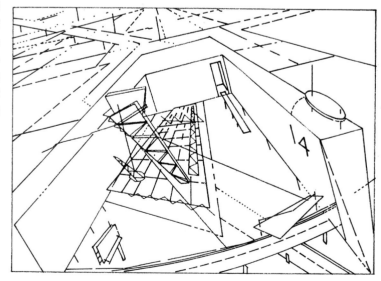

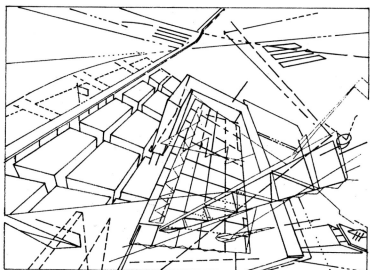

Our entry to the Amerika Gedenkbibliothek (A.E.G.) competition employs shark-like means to non-shark-like ends. Although the additions we propose appear to "violate" the existing library building, it is a division which unifies. While the exterior massing of the building appears visually incoherent from certain angles, it is in fact a harmonious totality; although its composition places emphasis on its brightly colored parts, the Amerika Gedenkbibliothek is a building which has a strict organization.

Within the context of the library's organization, wall-like forms take on an ambiguous expression. While they appear to be merely a gratuitous contemporary formal device in the service of fragmentation, the walls of the A.E.G. unify rather than divide. The Wall of Authors, which knifes into the original building, is inscribed with German authors on one side and American authors on the other. The act of using the circulation system engages the visitor in both the distinctness and the unity of the two sides of the wall, and by extension of American and German cultures. A hollow wall adjacent to the outdoor theater (expressed as a fallen shard) provides a subterranean link to the adjacent Jewish cemetery.

At the urban level the Amerika Gedenkbibliothek is also no mere "shark-like" exercise in formal manipulation. It represents rather than excludes its physical and historical context. Its apparently "fragmented or chaotic" composition is rather conceived as an intensification and knitting together of the random pattern of destruction and urban development of Berlin and, by extension, of contemporary urban society. A bronze wall to the right of the entry is aligned with the center of the circular Mehringplatz one quarter mile away. The skewed red wall reflects the orientation of the cemetery to which it provides access. The seemingly random pattern of paths criss-crossing the site stitch together existing routes adjacent to the site and reflect adjacent alignments.

We believe that inaccessible meaning may not be meaning at all and that an escalation of complex form (and criticism) may not address or empower anyone other than the already privileged. An "investigatory" architectural experiment in fragmentation may, therefore, disturb users and disrupt function without empowering them to reconsider their relationship to either society or its structure and artifact – architecture.

**FLORIAN/
WIERZBOWSKI**
model
**Amerika Gedenkbibliothek
Competition Project**
Berlin, Germany, 1989

Ours is, therefore, a division which clarifies. The composition of the A.E.G. is ambiguous, but legible. Although the forms of the building fragment, they do not dismember; they indicate rather than complete an order – the violation of the existing orders. The Wall of Authors directs visitors from the entry to reading rooms and stacks. A split section is used to maximize the physical and visual accessibility of the stacks to the public. What appears to be random fragmentation on the exterior is, therefore, in the service of internal order.

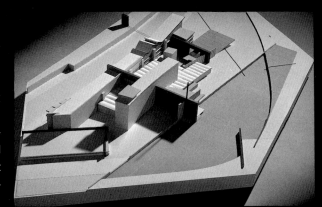

FLORIAN/
WIERZBOWSKI
axonometrics
Amerika Gedenkbibliothek
Competition Project
Berlin, Germany, 1989

While fragmentary asymmetrical modernism is thought to subvert monumentality, the A.E.G. is resolutely public: composed and monumental in the tradition of Dudok and Dutker. Although wounded, slashed and crumpled, the A.E.G. prevails as a ship of state: the emblem of a nation that wears its scars with courage and conviction.

So much of fragmentation is motivated by a kind of high moral "rude boy" mentality. The architects practicing it use it as a means to shock (usually called "critique"). We find this Roarkean avant-garde obsession with the supposed "new" to be limiting. To be avant garde is to be much more than a "bad boy" designer of freeze-dried explosions. With the eventual dilution of that architecture's unconventionality in its common use, its forms cease to subvert. We feel that the design of buildings might be infused with the desire to "delight" rather than the desire to disturb or challenge. "Terror" could be no more a cognitive disfunction.

The complex may in fact be simple. It seems probable that our perception of society as threatening in scale and complexity is an illusion and a question of scale. We may simply be unreceptive to change and ill-equipped to understand large-scale organizations in the process of development.

We purpose a violation that gains its power from ambiguity. The library is both investigatory and revelatory, accomodating and challenging, legible and non-legible, enigmatic and representational.

Paul Florian and Stephen Wierzbowski

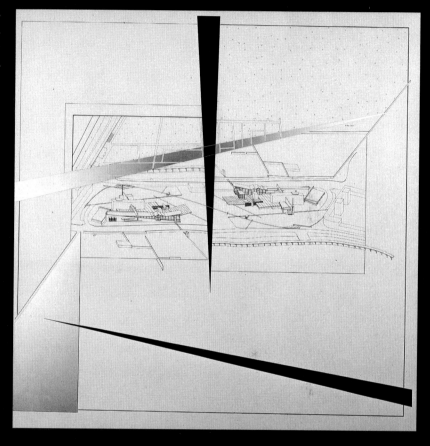

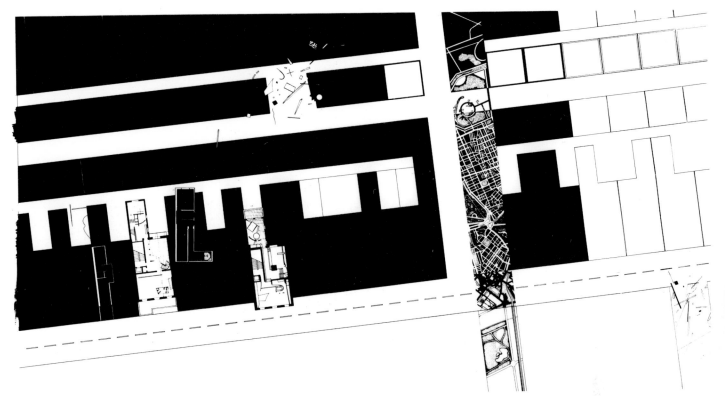

Zaha Hadid has undoubtedly taken the refinement of shards and sharks the furthest. Trained by Rem Koolhaas, and using the formal vocabulary of the Russian constructivists, Zaha Hadid creates "planetary architecture." Her student projects distilled modernism to its most abstract and ideal state, resembling both Malevich's suprematist space compositions and similar efforts by Theo van Doesburg. She next exploded these perfected planes, quite literally, in her drawings for the 59 Eaton Place Project of 1982. The Peak Competition, won in 1982, assembles these elements in an unstable way. Now one of the most copied projects of the last decade, the design proposes a series of simple, functional bars embedded in the steep hillside of its Hong Kong site. These bars are neither stacked nor aligned, but are thrown defiantly against nature, internally fragmented and never

ZAHA HADID
site and location plan
Apartment Conversion at 59 Eaton Place
London, England, 1982

ZAHA HADID
The Peak Competition Project
Hong Kong, 1983

presented as a whole. Hadid depicts these planes in a drawing reducing both the confusion of Hong Kong and the rocks above it to similar planes. This architecture takes on the basics of physical reality, and recrafts it. The "retooling" involves steel trusses and gridded surfaces that intersect tightly controlled functional cells, a technology gone haywire that exists only to take pleasure in defying gravity and convention.

Hadid also used this methodology in projects for Berlin and London which depict the city in an ever-more abstracted and skewed manner – the logical end point of the metropolis' development. She then layers plans and sections onto her supposed pro-

ject. Its very solidity is in question. Simultaneously enigmatic and confusing, Hadid's proposed shards have a menacing ambiguity threatening to destabilize our world. Her viewpoint and vision are expressed in drawings, and epitomized in *The World*, 1983, which broaches the realm of the cinematic. For Hadid, architecture as a representation of modernization's "unreality" is more closely aligned with cinema and television than other art forms, such as sculpture or rock and roll.[24]

The development of an architecture of shards and sharks is by now exhibiting four basic characteristics. First, Peter Wilson describes the tendency towards disappearance in terms of his own theoretical projects: "The subject of the project is the physicality of architecture and the ephemerality of the contemporary city, the evaporation of distance and matter through electronic technology, things are becoming invisible. The house is a black hole, an electronic shadow.... The house exists as its shadow, respectfully, fearfully, optimistically."[25] Second, some of the work absorbs itself in consumer culture, as evinced by the successful creation of a residential and commercial architectural style built with these shards and sharks. The third aspect of this work embraces either a cinematic or mythological narrative justifying its own existence. Last, there is a tendency towards technomorphism, and the acceptance that this explosion within the discipline leads to an "architectural third world war." These last two characteristics will be discussed next.

1. Koike, Mika, Motoi Masaki, Makoto Murata (Eds) *Kawamata*. Transl. by Junko Iwabuchi, Susan B. Klein, Lingua Guild, Inc. Tokyo: Gendaikikakushitsu Publishing, 1987.

2. For more recent work, see: Cook, Peter. *21 Years - 21 Ideas*. London: Architectural Association, 1985; for previous work, see: *Experimental Architecture*. New York: Universe Books, 1970.

3. Vannas, Dimitri, and Roland Cowan. "On a Kinetic Theory of Architecture." *Architectural Review*, V. 180, #1074, August, 1986, pp. 62-67.

4. Cook, Peter. "Austria Vienna: Graz". *The Architectural Review*, December, 1988, pp-23-26.

5. Domenig, Guenther. *Stone House at Steindorf*. Drawings and Models. Klagenfurt, Austria: Ritter Verlag, 1988.

6. Ibid.

7. Krischanitz, Adolf, Oskar Putz, and Margherita Krischanitz. *Haus in Sallmansdorf. Architektur Farbe Fotografie*. Vienna: Wiener Secession, 1989

8. Prix, Wolf, and Helmut Swiczinsky. *Coop Himmelblau. The Power of the City*. Transl. by Robert Hahn, Roswitha Prix, Jo Steinbauer and Edda Zimmermann. Darmstadt: Verlag der George Buechner Buchhandlung, 1988, p. 95.

9. Lecture by Wolf Prix at the University of California at Los Angeles, May 4, 1989, and discussions with author, January-May, 1989.

10. Ibid.

11. Honold, Reinhards, and Wolfgang Poeschl. "Arch 13 (Bar) Innsbruck; Dragonwing." *Architectural Review*, V. 180, #1074, August, 1986, pp. 52-56.

12. Wilson, Peter. *Bridgebuildings + The Shipshape*. London: The Architectural Association. 1984.

13. Shinohara, Kazuo. "Chaos and Machine." *The Japan Architect*, #373, May, 1988, pp. 25-32.

14. Shinohara, Kazuo. "Tokyo Institute of Technology Centennial Hall." *The Japan Architect*, op.cit., pp. 6-24.

15. Bognar, Botand. "An Art and Architecture of Fragmentation: The New Urban Architecture of Japan," in *The New Japanese Architecture*, New York: Rizzoli, 1990.

16. Angelo Tarlazzi House. *Icon*, May, 1987, pp. 30-36.

17. See also: Bognar, Botand (ed.) *Japanese Architecture*. London: Academy Editions, 1988.

18. Dietsch, Deborah K. "Prince of Darkness. Three Buildings by Atsushi Kitagawara + ILCD, Inc., Architect" *Architectural Record*, Vol. 176, No. 2, February, 1988, pp. 108-121. See also: Bognar, Botand (ed.) *Japanese Architecture*. London: Academy Editions, 1988.

19. Buchanan, Peter. "Catalan Constructivism." *Architectural Review*, October, 1987, pp. 57-60.

20. Want, Winfried (Ed.) *Alvaro Siza: Figures and Configurations: Buildings and Projects 1986-1988*. New York: Rizzoli International Publications, 1988.

21. "High Prow." *World of Interiors*, October, 1988, pp. 235-245.

22. Central Office of Architecture. "Los Angeles and the Curse of Bigness." *Offramp* V. 1, #2, Spring, 1989.

23. Central Office of Architecture. *Recombinant Images in Los Angeles*. Los Angeles: Los Angeles Forum for Architecture and Urban Design, 1989.

24. Futagawa, Yukio. *Zaha M. Hadid. (G.A. Architect 5)*. Tokyo: A.D.A. Edita, 1986. See also: Hadid, Zaha. *Planetary Architecture*. London: The Architectural Association, 1985.

25. Wilson, Peter L. Competition Entry Description. *The Japan Architect*, March 1983, pp. 8-9.

DAVID IRELAND
meeting rooms
Marin Center for the Arts
Marin Headlands, California, 1986
Photo: Aaron Betsky

MASQUES, MESSAGES
AND TEXTS

To some architects building is itself suspect. Any creation of an autonomous object complies with and reaffirms the social and economic status quo, suppressing and distorting all other possible orders. Architectural forms, our built language, voice the bad conscience of their underlying structure, feigning truth, like words which gloss over their social implications. But a facade or floor plan seems only a pale reflection of the real structure of a building. One confronts a double distortion: what you see is the false mask of a building, distorted by an act of construction that is also repressive. Finally, the very existence of the architectural object dissimulates the abstract language of space and time, the complex social and economic orders out of which it is made. The textualists believe that the privileging of the object, and of an architecture based on this idolatry, must be overthrown. By exposing otherwise repressed structures of architecture and manipulating them to refuse resolution, the textualists reveal architecture's internal conflicts and their inability to create a truly stable structure. Textualists also utilize alternative systems of coherence, such as geometry, allegory or narrative, to create an architecture that resists its traditional role, instead becoming an integral part of our daily performance in the world. Architecture becomes fragmented into sets, cues or machines, tools uncovering or offering a possible way of making sense out of our world.

DAVID IRELAND
500 Capp Street
(David Ireland House)
San Francisco, California, 1978
(Situation in 1989)
Photo: Aaron Betsky

Much of this work is extremely theoretical, seemingly far removed from the activities traditionally understood as architecture. The work of David Ireland, a San Francisco sculptor, is one exception. A decade ago, Ireland purchased a nineteenth-century house in a run-down neighborhood. Rather than reorganizing the space with additional forms, he uncovered the accumulated layers of wallpaper, tile, and paint from the surfaces – its history – and sealed them with shellac. He next removed the molding from the windows, doors, and walls to expose the interaction of materials and mechanisms narrating the building's operations. Ireland placed "still lifes" of objects he had used, the appropriated debris of consumerism, throughout his home. The house has become a stage set for a daily performance. This direct, physical, and powerful deconstructive attitude towards architecture transforms the house into a revealing text for a daily performance.

Most of those concerned with architecture as text work much more abstractly. Since the design of House X, 1975, **Peter Eisenman** continues to feed the structures of architecture back into themselves (in the manner of a computer feedback loop), overlaying, colliding, and extruding multiple ordering principles in order to create complicated layers of possible coherence, all unresolved. After his engagement with pure geometry, he moved towards projects such as the Romeo and Juliet House of 1976 and appropriated notions of scalar geometry and mapping.[1] Using a formula developed by the scientist Benoit Mandelbrot, which determines the "self-sameness" or autonomous replication inherent in certain figures, he mapped

plans of vast territories over each other. This technique questioned architecture's relation to a "normal scale" and "problematized" the concept of human perspective.[2] The 1989 Wexner Center for the Visual Arts at Ohio State University introduces the purposefully arbitrary. A walkway's disruptive diagonal incorporates the grid of the city into the layout of the university by following the directional of an airport landing strip several miles away. Repressed features of this site, where an armory once stood, were resurrected and built as fragments, as valid and complete as the abstract geometries and arbitrary incisions which shape this complex and unresolved building.[3]

Eisenman's most recent work seems to become almost mystical in its search for repressed systems. The organizing principle of his project for the

PETER EISENMAN
Wexner Center
for the Visual Arts
at Ohio State University
Columbus, Ohio, 1989
Photo: ARTOG

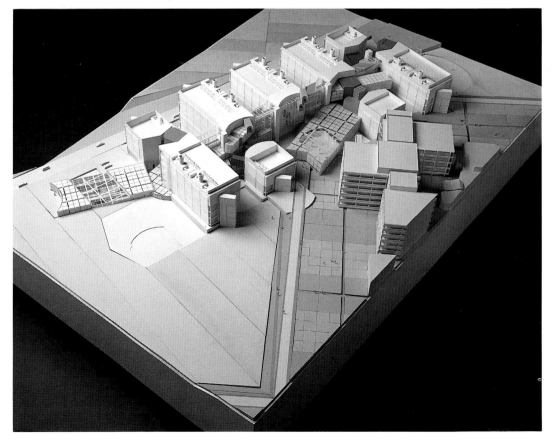

PETER EISENMAN
model
Frankfurt Biozentrum Project
Frankfurt, Germany, 1987
Photo: Dick Frank

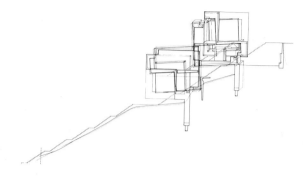

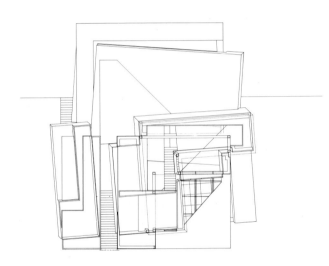

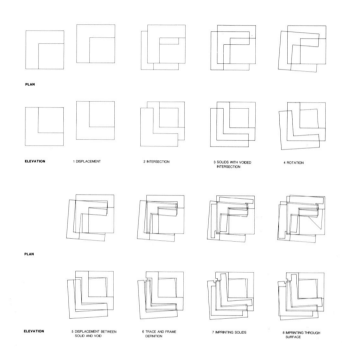

PETER EISENMAN
diagrams and sections
Guardiola House
Puerto de Santa Maria
Cadiz, Spain, 1989

PLAN

ELEVATION

| 1 DISPLACEMENT | 2 INTERSECTION | 3 SOLIDS WITH VOIDED INTERSECTION | 4 ROTATION |

PLAN

ELEVATION

| 5 DISPLACEMENT BETWEEN SOLID AND VOID | 6 TRACE AND FRAME DEFINITION | 7 IMPRINTING SOLIDS | 8 IMPRINTING THROUGH SURFACE |

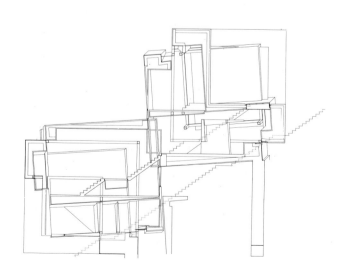

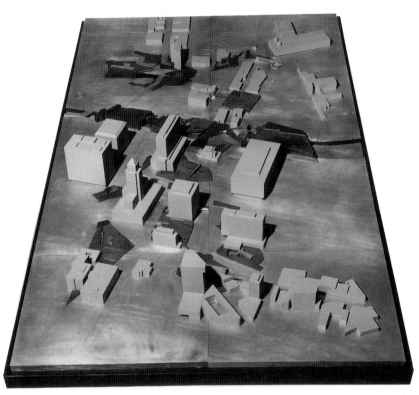

Biology Center of the J. W. Goethe University of Frankfurt, 1987, is the DNA chain. Eisenman used its physical configuration and methods of growth – replication, transcription, and translation – to blow up the forms of the program. Fractal geometry enabled him to create a building which could "become complicit with the discipline that it houses," rather than "representing" biology. To safeguard architecture from disappearing completely into this science, Eisenman then meshed fractal geometry with that of the trellis on the back of Goethe's house, "infecting" one geometry or text with an equally available one. Refusing to judge how the university's name, function, or purpose should guide the design, Eisenman proposed a series of transcriptions, translations, and replications creating their own text. This series resembled a building, or a series of architectural investigations with functional delimitations translated into three-dimensional form. Eisenman seems to be seeking the key to life before language and logic, and, at the same time, finding a language of code at that moment of beginning. This is a spatial and linguistic code, an architecture. The feeling of alienation is thus anchored deep within our bodies. Eisenman has offered the final victory of language and a linguistic model of architecture.[4] Architecture can now only become Derrida's *chora*: a receptacle between place and object, the trace of humanity written on sifting sand.[5]

Eisenman almost singularly affirms a positivistic faith in architecture's ability to create multiple, grafted, and infected texts whose very lack of traditional coherence makes them valid operating manuals in a world of modernization. Most architects are more troubled by repressive acts and artificial texts that we construct with our social activities. The Los Angeles firm of AKS Runo dug underneath the city surface to find its "metapolis" – potential orders which the city could next develop in a frag-mentary and enigmatic fashion. Their procedure is to "ignore the site and ignore architecture... there is no such thing as architecture." Instead they begin with an invented abstract grid, and "intertextual" references to other disciplines such as art or literature. Although these texts are as valid and inherent in our experience of the city as any others, they are outside of, or on the margins of, accepted methods of composing the city. They are experienced as conscious irritants, interruptions in our under-standing of the city, which appear as fragments popping up through the surface of the streets, inscribed lines and indecipherable objects placed within, through, or in front of buildings. This alternate text continually comments on the "normal" text of the city. According to the members of AKS Runo, the logic of the new text is based on "the dimension of our time" (which is not necessarily the third dimension). The physical reality of the proposal is neither object, nor surface, nor structure, although it does indi-

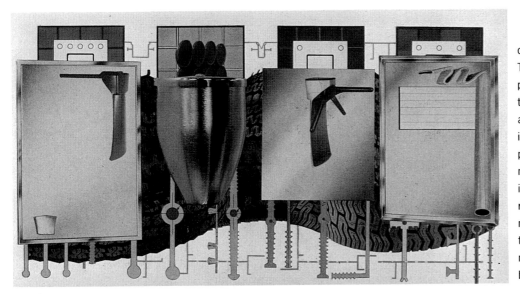

cate such possible directions. The "metapolis" of AKS Runo is a possible text to be read between the lines of everyday existence, an alternate poetics. Its violent interruption of the city and purposeful irresolution suggest a metaphor of modernization, an interpretation that AKS Runo resists, preferring to see their methodology as existing "beyond the modern," since it confronts neither technology nor change, but crafts alternate texts.[6]

English-born **Ben Nicholson**, who currently works in Chicago, like the partners in AKS Runo, studied with Daniel Libeskind, and now obsessively investigates the smallest objects of consumer society for hidden texts of modernization. Working "on a microscale" with pieces of machinery or fragments of mass-produced objects, he discovers allusions to a much larger world, condensed in the form and upon the object's surface. A section of a telephone answering machine button, for instance, might reveal the figure of a man. He

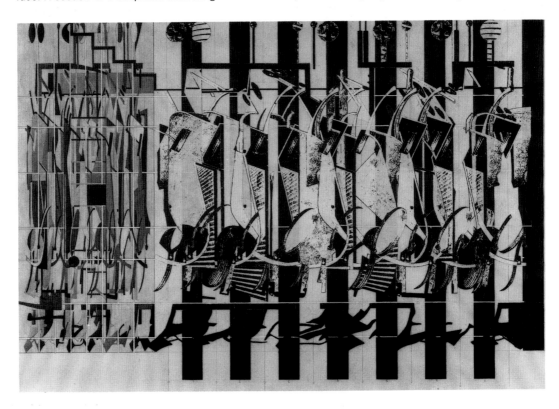

captures these discoveries by xeroxing and collaging his drawings and using the "translations" to construct an architecture built of now-incomprehensible notations. To Nicholson, this archaeological method provides a means of "forcing the status quo to present itself to you" so that it can be mapped out and distorted. The sheer weight and complexity of the instructions, producing highly engineered objects, provide a creative space in the thick layers of inscribed systems. The incidental, hidden text of the processes of production and consumption rather than architecture become the originating text.[7] The Appliance House, composed of these texts, depicts the end result of his continual and obsessive collecting, transcribing, xeroxing and three-dimensional translation. Using texts that are both absurd and sensible, he bases the room on an alternative to the surburban home. He invents activities which, instead of defining normative behavior and a clear and easily recognizable shelter, provide dangerous and surrealistic juxtapositions of shape and suggestions. Nicholson destabilizes the basic notion of exile and retreat in the myth of suburbia.[8]

Raoul Bunschoten's projects – condensed and framed

maps of our society – work on a macroscale. Beginning with Spinoza's Garden Project, 1985, he interprets architecture as a rupture or wound in the surface of the earth – a "trauma." Like Derrida's pharmekon,[9] this trauma allows us to construct an artificial life, and also divides, fragments, and otherwise defeats our sense of the world around us.

Architecture appears as an artificial continuation of the project of fragmentation and connection. But, by representing itself endlessly and enigmatically, it is liberated, becoming trauma itself. Bunschoten proposes to build this representation, rather than hiding it as some hidden meaning or invisible motor force.

RAOUL BUNSCHOTEN
model
Spinoza's Garden
Amsterdam, The Netherlands,
1986
Photo: Hélène Binet

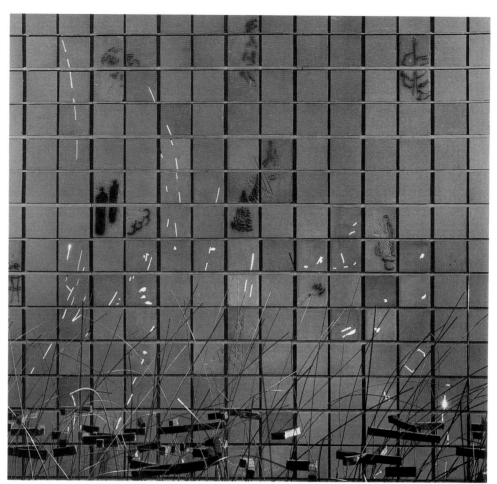

In Apeiron: or Chaos Embodied, a project for the center of Berlin completed in 1988, Bunschoten proposes an "annunciation." "The surface of the picture is like a model, an embodied analogy of a larger complexity." To a world of chaos, disconnection, and incomprehensible forms, Bunschoten announces "a field of spermatozoa, seeds of the urban space." It is a "parasite… new land," the potential for architecture.[10] This architecture is an inscribed set of lines connecting rocks, as arbitrary as a passing cloud, and, like all urban space, framed by cultural preconceptions and built forms. Bunschoten creates clay and string models, mapping out incisions or lines of connection in the world's text. These maps are critical rather than direct commentaries: "By making an object, you question everything else."[11] Bunschoten's 1989 project in Asperen, the Netherlands, was made up of a ring of cast spheres becoming progressively smaller and more translucent as they sliced through the earth. This is a microcosm of our universe, an opening up of the earth, and a new text commenting on its own activities – the "negative" plate of the book of life.

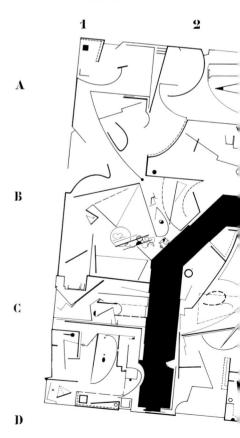

The more cinematic investigations of **Mojdeh Baratloo** and **Clifton J. Balch** present a counterpoint to a passive acceptance of fragmentation and the violation of all texts. After exploring an industrial section of New York, they plotted out their experience of the place, and then used this wholly arbitrary "map

A5

B4 B6

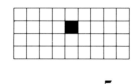

of exploration" to construct episodic and evocative interruptions. Fearful of the city, Baratloo and Balch map out, re-enact, and then represent the condition of being lost in an unintelligible world. Their proposed labyrinth augments the existing urban one. Composed of associations and invented histories, embodied in photographs and allusions to Italo Calvino, it proposes a continual and experiential cartography through which one might not only discover an architectural reality, but continually rewrite it.[12]

C5

MOJDEH BARATLOO,
CLIFTON J. BALCH
plan section
Angst: Cartography
Brooklyn, New York, 1989

B 5

3　　4　　5　　6　　7　　8　　9

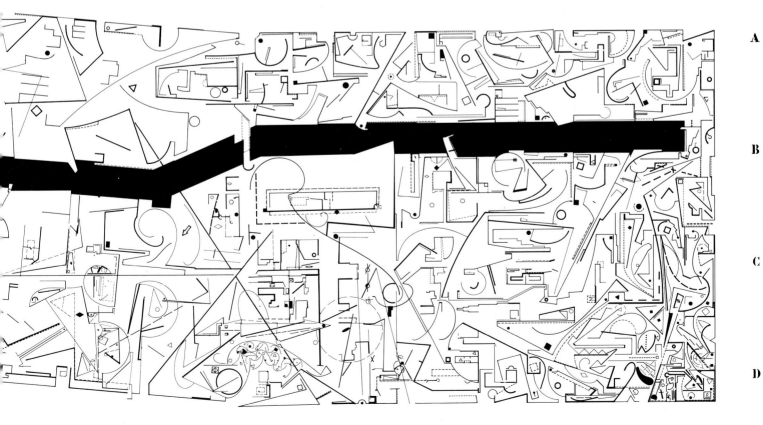

A

B

C

D

3　　4　　5　　6　　7　　8　　9

NIGEL COATES
Arkalbion Project
London, England, 1984

This kind of activity now occurs in virtually every urban area of the Western world, and has roots in the work of John Hejduk as well as that of Bernard Tschumi during his involvement with the Architectural Association. One of Tschumi's students, **Nigel Coates**, took over his teacher's "unit" and proceeded to make a "literary" architecture. For Coates, architecture must become a built analogy of experience – of necessity impressionistic and malleable, projecting both something yet to be realized and a filmic vision that reorganizes existing reality. His architecture, embodied in such pro-

jects as Arkalbion, is composed of photographs and expressionistic doodles providing a fragmented narrative for a possible city that would replace a large section of London.[13] This narrative becomes an autonomous alternative to building, a chance for the individual to remake the world in a fragmentary fashion: "narratives are no longer based on any reference to the world but on the very conditions that the place is made of, its cranes, its processes, its images... Everything you do there is touched by the resonant effects of utterly ordinary things...narrative break-up."[14]

Steven Holl, in his Porto Vittorio, Milan, project, 1987, proposes a much more romantically resolved version of such a narrative architecture. Holl first denies the coherence of any architectural objects or abstract systems outside of direct perception. The complexities of urban experience are such that "time, matter, space, and light intermesh with the activities of the modern city, forcing us to reconsider assumptions of urban planning. He instead proposes a "three-dimensional sectional approach that gives primary

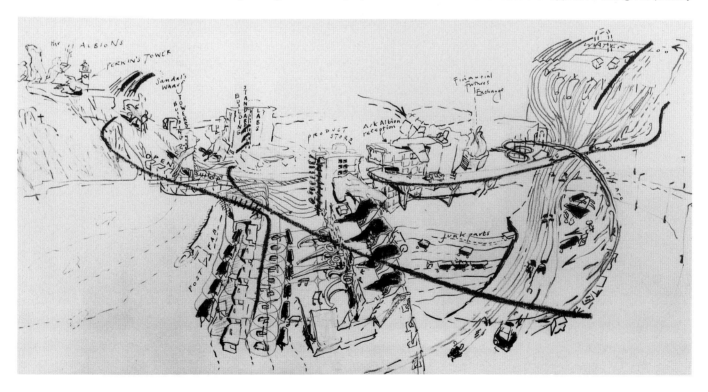

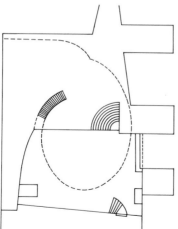

importance to the view of perambulatory residents who traverse shifting ground planes, experiencing the city from multiple frames of reference." Such a "parallax" arrangement breaks through the rationality of program, material, function, and all other organizations of experience attempting to control and order our lives. To build this sectional destabilization of architecture, he proposes using "semi-automatic programming," a form of inventive design relying on intuitive and associational impulses building "the hidden text" of whatever program or site the architect encounters.

In the Milan project, a Disneyland-like promenade passes through lakes, hotels, office blocks, and fragmentary monuments, each with a particular name, story, and composition based on certain associations the architect has with the site. The lake refers to the original name of the site (Largo Marinia d'Italia). The hotel is only for unhappy lovers, and the bureaucratic office tower has a section whose fluctuations alter in accordance with changing political needs. The actual forms deny a stable ground plane, cutting through and rising from the skin of the earth like the forms of Bunschoten, but are clad with a stripped-down and fragmentary form of modernism.

MICHAEL WEBB
Temple Island study
The Bride
Hedley, England,1989

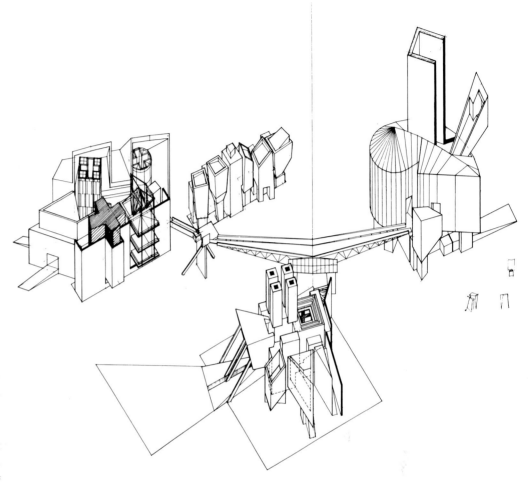

This is Hannes Meyer gone mad; within the ramblings of the madman's hallucinations lie an alternative to the deadening and oppressive effects of the modern city.

The Temple Island Project by **Michael Webb** works with much more abstract and evocative narrative disjunction. This text/design traces a day at the boat races through a series of watercolor drawings and pseudo-scientific drawings. The images present a continually shifting perspective based on both expository and scientific ordering properties associated with architecture. The text moves from an evocation of childhood to an "idiocy" meant to mimic the *idiot savant* – the computer – liberating the flow of human experience.[15]

In addition to abstracting language as a system, or creating grand narratives beyond built form, some architects follow the lead of John Hejduk and create architecture as masques. For the Piazza Navona in Rome, **Danelle Guthrie** and **Tom Buresh** proposed a project narrating the story of a city whose text has become illegible: the decaying monuments of the city are disconnected from the lives of those inhabiting them. Guthrie and Buresh propose sending the inhabitants forced out of their collapsing homes away in an ark, a floating building that seems to act as a funnel of light and services. Their belongings remain behind as witnesses to their habitation of the Piazza. A room containing all of the maps of the city, which are

collected and read, also remains, preserving the memory of the city. As the real architecture disappears, a story can be told about it. Its physical reality exists as a series of highly distorted cones, stairs, and cylinders which twist and turn out of plans, sections, and elevations revolving around each other on the page. Guthrie and Buresh create a highly sophisticated sequence of architectural spaces, but the oddness of their forms marks them forever as stories told about architecture.

Other architects make pavilions which, as performance machines, recompose our world with an alternative syntax. After the break-up of narrative and the disappearance of coherent forms, only

TOM BURESH,
DANELLE GUTHRIE
ark
**Roma in Restauro:
Observatories**
Rome, Italy, 1988

episodes from the text remain to be constructed and acted out, such as **John Whiteman**'s Divisible by 2 project, 1988. This ostensibly functionless small pavilion, an empty cube, presents an alternative to the most basic "essay form of architecture." The metal grid of the structure hints at stability, yet only as scaffolding – as a possibility for building rather than enclosing walls. The walls hanging from this scaffolding are movable metal panels and plywood partitions. The doors, scaled according to different standards for men and women, as prescribed in *Architectural Graphic Standards*,[16] shift by each other without quite meeting. Their burned and rubbed surfaces seem to have been tortured by an attempt to aestheticize them, making them into "skins." The translucent floor of the empty interior is embedded with cigarette butts, bolts, and other leftovers from the construction process. The whole pavilion thus functions as a constructed rather than written metaphor for building itself. Only the "subject," or user as "performer," remains.

To read the text one must become part of the pavilion's architectural functioning, using its doors, frames, and window/floor. Whiteman dissolved architecture into pure text, distilled to a script for a performance.[17]

The German firm **Formalhaut** has long been concerned with such scripts. One of their first projects consisted of taking apart a Volkswagen bus and transforming the movable habitation into a stack of planes or pictures (Caravan, 1987). They also covered buildings (Rendezvous, 1986), people (Sporthalle, 1986) and cows (Kuhproject, 1986) with corrugated translucent sheets

FORMALHAUT
Double Knight Game
Frankfurt, Germany, 1989
Photo: Götz Stockmann

which distorted the facade or figure, forcing one to confront them as strange apparitions.[18] The 1988 Chess Game proposed looking at social relations in the modern city as a chess game, a highly structured intersection of chance, hierarchy, and strategy. Constructing a grid of translucent cylinders, they suggested

considering the grid as the prototype of habitations for individuals. This forces us to see architecture as a distorting plane, and to acknowledge its role in cultural intervention rather than connection. Architecture returns to "square one," a potential cultural construct, an inventor of meaning.[19]

New York architects Jesse Reiser and Nanako Umemoto constructed a pavilion as a reading machine. Within a metal frame, a chaise longue is suspended, inviting one to read a plate which has been layered with language and then sanded down. Reiser and Umemoto first construct a layering of words in

FORMALHAUT
Cow Project
Vogelsberg/Hessen, Germany, 1986
Photo: Alexander Beck

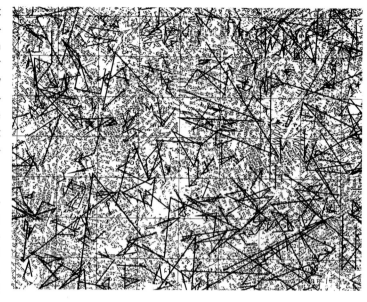

order to reveal various texts that are then blown up, mathematically manipulated, and inscribed on an "engendering plate." Their machine for reading is the new "theater of the world," a sculptural object, a machine, a piece of furniture, and a portable set for our own performance of reading the world.[20]

Diller + Scofidio use performance architecture as an incisive tool to fragment and alter everyday activities. The absurdity and violence of clichés and commonplace elements are revealed in the process of constructing a ritualistic representation culminating in an offering of possibilities. Their Delay in Glass project comments on Marcel Duchamp's *Large Glass*. Although the original work successfully de-individualizes desire, mapping it within fragmented icons of a diffused and mechanized culture that correctly interprets the essentially technological nature of human actions, including desire, it also preserves myths of separation and male domination. The Large Glass can also be read as a representation of conventional modern architecture, perpetuating the myth of Platonic desire for an unattainable idea. The desire, clothed in a modernistic garb, is still framed within the ordered and functioning world of cultural

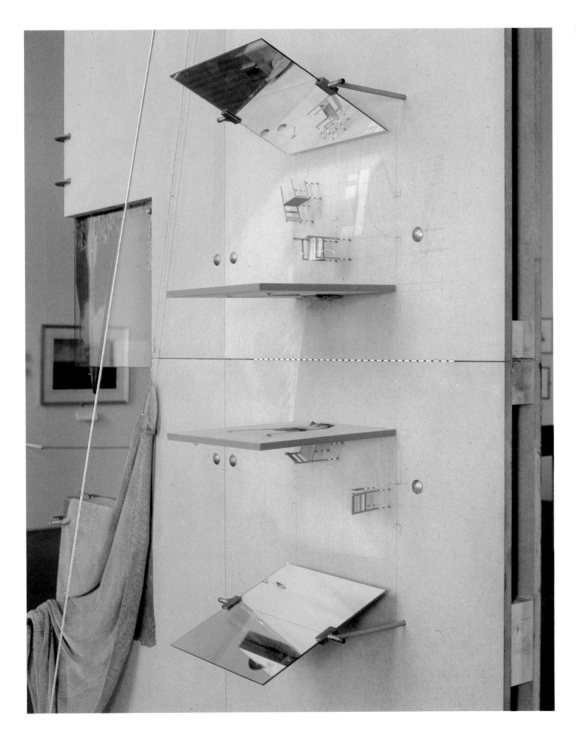

DILLER + SCOFIDIO
Urban Suburban Rural
Windows
XVII Triennale
Milan, Italy, 1986
Photo: D. Rosselli

DILLER + SCOFIDIO
A Delay in Glass,
or The Rotary Notary
and His Hot Plate,
a Probe into the Instability
of Gender
New York, New York, 1987

representation. Diller + Scofidio activate and play out these differences with interactive generic figures that, along with various fragmentary objects, rotate around the stage. Top and bottom, violence and attraction, male and female are purposefully confused, thus "dis-integrating the singular in favor of the more fertile multiple."[21]

The works of Diller + Scofidio go beyond performance art in their direct confrontation with architecture. They consider architecture to be a set of stable and unquestioned assumptions needing alteration. In constructing a highly articulated machine, a set of fragmented and self-reflexive mirrors based on the window, the most absent of architectural elements, they remarked: "The window reconciles the original violation of the wall.... The window is a legal limit that tempts the uninvited. The window is an apparatus that conspires with other machines to homogenize the weather. The window resists horizontal load and breeds dust."[22]

In 1987, Diller + Scofidio constructed a Drawing Room in the Capp Street Project in San Francisco. This project "designated a 'domestic field' between the skin of the house and the skin of the body." They next addressed rituals of property, etiquette, intimacy, and narcissism: progressively defining the self by means of division and withdrawal, stripping away society to discover the body. This set up an environment of destabilization: the property line becomes a cut through the house and furniture, the dining room table is suspended near the ceiling, and a double bed splits in two and rotates through space. Function, stable space, and all behavioral cues dictated by architecture have been actively subverted. Later projects reconstruct fragments of this architectural discipline as mirrors or gates which remain contradictory, detached, and enigmatic. We rediscover only the body as corps rather than the body as

DILLER + SCOFIDIO
bed
the withDrawing Room:
versions and subversions
65 Capp Street
San Francisco, California, 1987

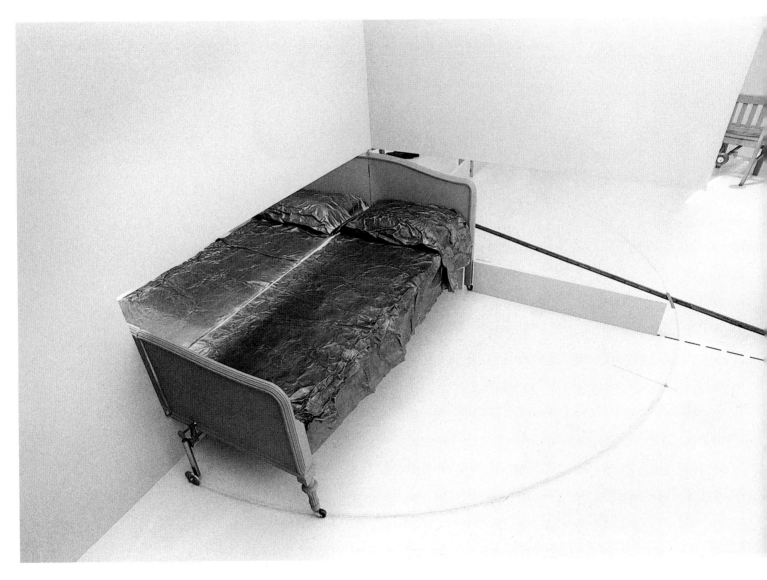

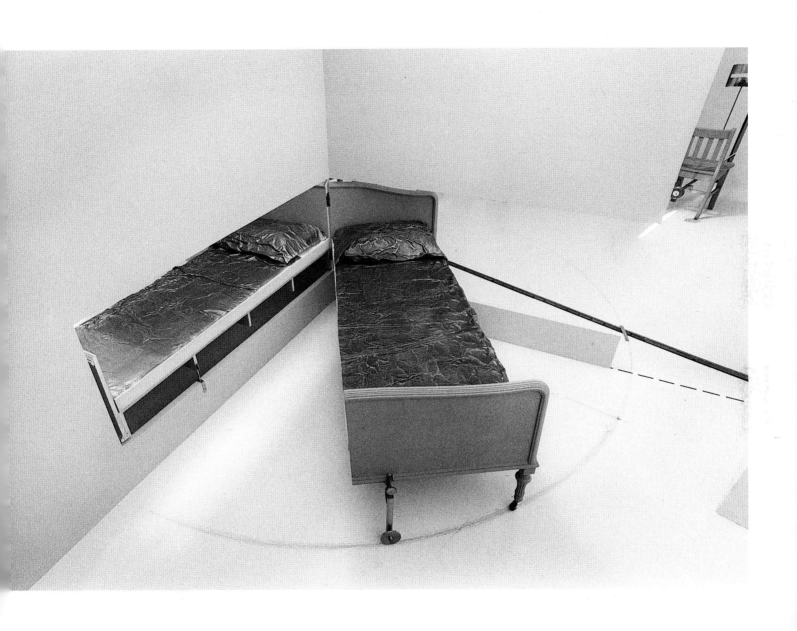

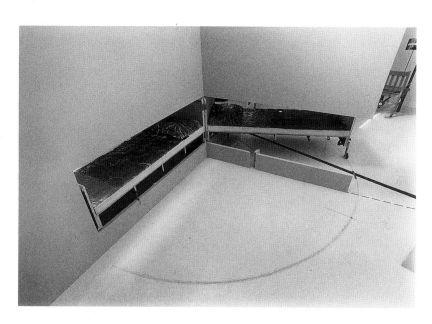

self or flesh. It is as an empty object free to attract social relationships.[23] Diller + Scofidio erase language and all architecture built on language in order to gain this freedom. To construct the necessarily self-violating elements of a technological game, architecture becomes a performance promising the liberating possibility of a world beyond logic, language, architecture or self.

DILLER + SCOFIDO
bed
the withDrawing Room:
versions and subversions
65 Capp Street
San Francisco, California, 1987

1. Eisenman, Peter. "Moving Arrow, Eros and Other Errors." Vergani, Gianmarco (Ed). *Precis 6. The Journal of the Columbia University Graduate School of Architecture and Urban Planning. The Culture of Fragments. Notes on the Question of Order in a Pluralistic World,* pp. 139-144. This text was published in many different locations—as are most of Eisenman's texts. The most lavish production is a "folio" of the same title published by the Architectural Association in 1986.

2. For a clear explication of Eisenman's working method during this period, see: Marvel, Jonathan Jova (Ed.). *Investigations in Architecture. Eisenman Studios at the GSD: 1983-85.* Cambridge, MA: Harvard University Graduate School of Design, 1986.

3. Arnell, Peter, and Ted Bickford. *A Center for the Visual Arts. The Ohio State University Competition.* New York: Rizzoli International Publications, 1984.

4. Eisenman, Peter. "Biology Center for the J.W. Goethe University of Frankfurt, Frankfurt am Main, 1987." *Assemblage* #5, February, 1988, pp. 29-50.

5. Eisenman, Peter. *Guardiola House.* Berlin: Aedes Gallery, 1989. This recalls Michel Foucault's argument for the disappearance of the very notion of humanity: "one can certainly wager that man would be erased, like a face drawn in sand at the edge of the sea" (p. 387). *The Order of Things. An Archaeology of the Human Sciences.* New York: Vintage Books, 1973 (1966).

6. Conversation with Bahram Shirdel, Andrew Zago, William Taylor (Principals, AKS Runo), Los Angeles, California, March 15, 1988.

7. Conversation with Ben Nicholson, Chicago, Illinois, May 11, 1989.

8. Nicholson, Ben. "The Appliance House." Unpublished manuscript.

9. Cf. Preface.

10. Bunschoten, Raoul. "Apeiron: or Chaos Embodied. A Project for the Center of Berlin." Unpublished manuscript, 1988.

11. Conversation with Nicholson, op.cit.

12. Baratloo, Mojdeh, and Clifton J. Balch. *Angst: Cartography.* New York: SITES/Lumen Books, 1989.

13. Coates, Nigel. *Arkalbion and Six Other Projects.* London: The Architectural Association, 1984.

14. Coates, Nigel. "Narrative Break-Up." Coates, Nigel (Ed.) *The Discourse of Events. Themes 3.* London: The Architectural Association, 1983, pp. 12-17, p. 17.

15. Webb, Michael. *Temple Island. A Study by Michael Webb.* London: The Architectural Assocation, 1987.

16. Packard, Robert T. (Ed.) Ramsey/Sleeper *Architectural Graphic Standards. Seventh Edition.* New York: John Wiley & Sons, 1981.

17. Whiteman, John. "Divisible by 2." *Assemblage* #7, October, 1988, pp. 43-56.

18. Cook, Peter. "Formalhaut. 2 Architects and Sculptor from Frankfurt." *Stroll* #6/7, 1988, pp. 34-39.

19. Formalhaut. *Double Knight Game.* Darmstadt: Verlag der Georg Buechner Buchhandlung, 1989.

20. See also--"Reiser & Umemoto." *The Architectural Review,* February, 1989, pp. 59-61; Reiser, Jesse, and Nanako Umemoto. "Globe Theater." Walczak, Marek, et.al. *The London Project.* New York: Princeton Architectural Press, 1989, Chapter 2.

21. McAnulty, Robert. "Diller+Scofidio." *Investigations 23.* Philadelphia: Institute of Contemporary Art, 1989.

22. Diller, Elizabeth, and Ricardo Scofidio. "Inside-Out: The Window on the Garden." Teyssot, Georges. *Interior Landscapes.* Trans. by C.H. Evans. New York: Electa Editrice/Rizzoli International Publications, 1987, pp. 66-70.

23. Diller, Elizabeth, and Ricardo Scofidio. *bodybuildings. architectural facts and fictions. Diller+Scofidio.* New York: Storefront for Art and Architecture, 1987.

LEBBEUS WOODS
Inverted Tower
and Bridge Living-Laboratories,
Sector 8571, Quadrant 1
Underground Berlin Project
Berlin, Germany, 1988

UTOPIAS,
DYSTOPIAS, HETEROTOPIAS

A utopian belief is central both to the modern movement and to any justification
or critique of its process. The ever-elusive utopian vision of total release,
effected by those mechanisms that place the good continually further out of reach,
even when it becomes its opposite – a dystopian vision of self-destruction –
is the end game of a teleology of reduction, rationalization, and abstraction. Both
a perfect world and a perfect destruction require a perfect, ideal architecture.
Yet this secular world demands an architecture not of heaven or hell, but of fact.
Thus the modern movement is still enthralled by the Howard Rourkian image
of a heroic builder, yet all possible built perfections are perpetually cancelled by
human activity. Furthermore, any system conceived of in the post-Heisenbergian
world is by nature incomplete, and any actual construction will violate the conceptual system's purity. Yet, although the U.S. is littered with failed utopias, tragic
attempts at expressing total order – from Burnham in Chicago to the Lindsay
administration in New York – the *New Mythologists* still assert that architecture
is a mythic activity. It constructs another world whose location and relation
to the past, present, and future are unknowable. To posit that world as analogy,
commentary, or critique requires simultaneously realizing that it is unrealizable.[1]

Ron Herron, a leading figure
in Archigram, proposed various
pod-like structures allowing
inhabitants to roam through a
mysterious arcadia, unconfined
by the city's social and physical
constraints.[2] Michael Sorkin's
city is pure energy. For each of
these visions there are countless
other projects to liberate us from
the constraints of gravity, perspective, climate control, style,
and every other imaginable convention in order to send us zoom-
ing off into a better world.

Although the term utopia origi-
nated in myth,[3] the model for

such an activity, and therefore
for many of its forms, comes
from film. From *The Shape of
Things to Come* to *2001: A
Space Odyssey* to *Star Wars*,
our culture has nourished itself
with images of better, or at least
more advanced, worlds to come.
Some of the most imaginative
architecture of the last several
decades, which is of course
overwhelmingly technological in
nature, has been constructed for
film. Architects can project
themselves beyond the current
state of modernization into the
world of *Star Trek*, *Blade Runner*, *Alien*, or *Outland*. These

movies make us believe that
technology will liberate us completely from earth, gravity, scale
and any traditional patterns of
social bonding. Yet they also
present the possibility that technology will develop into an isolated and menacing phenomenon,
creating small pockets of another such world – a destructive
parasite on reality. While the
abstracted, flowing interior
world of *Blade Runner* continues
Frank Lloyd Wright's idealistic
forms – Usonia transposed to a
dark new century – the outside
is a dramatic hell of refinery-like
spaces and Piranesian tunnels

at the base of immeasurably tall pyramidal skyscrapers. In *Batman*, Gotham City is a high tech neo-Gothic nightmare whose romantic forms have all the force of *King's Views of New York*. Yet the hero lives in baronial splendor in a clearly recognizable mansion. The realms of consumption and production have been segregated in all of these visions, their dialectic more resolved than any Marxist revolution – cut and spliced into seamlessness. The final ideal of modern architecture might be to build this seamless Hegelian *aufhebung*.

These utopian worlds are compelling. They present us with spacecraft interiors with huge vaulted halls, endless corridors, and either vertiginous spaces bridged by small metallic tentacles or limitless ethereal spaces. Their perfected architecture has become completely interiorized, infinite, and indistinguishable from its technological context.

Some architects remain content to receive inspiration from these visions; others actively participate in establishing such worlds. The 1960s visions of Archigram, Superstudio, and Constant still have followers. The 1985 competition "A Style for the year 2001" produced a vast array of responses, almost all sharing a

belief in continuing the development of modernism's abstracting, reductivist tendencies. Some used collage and "explosionistic" styles to the point that

film still of barracks
Outland
1981
Copyright © by The Ladd Company

film still of rooftop
Blade Runner
Warner Bros. © Copyright 1982
Ladd Company

they became forcefields, suspended globes, or endless cities – indistinguishable from the simulatory abilities of technology.[4]

Craig Hodgetts, a former car designer turned architect, designs sets for visionary films and commercials. His 1986 designs for a car commercial feature a completely metallic city – a rationalist set of silvery and monotonous blocks and towers. The miniature metropolis conveys both the excitement of perfection and its overwhelming uniformity. A subsequent commercial for Wang computers destroys any reference to a stable groundplane, context, or structure. The computer liberates the workplace to the point that it literally disappears. The proposed film *Ecotopia* expresses Hodgetts' most visionary design. Based on Ernest Callenbach's novel, this film envisions a world completely based on technology developed to the point that it ceases to rape the landscape and deform social relationships. Instead, it translates natural resources, leaving the energizing sun and the cultivated soil intact. It becomes a social enabler that transforms the world into a collective of craftsmen. Hodgetts' architecture gives form to this utopia. It maintains an underlying order of gridded blocks and trellises, but strips them down so that they seem incomplete and resemble armatures for sunscreens. A bewildering variety of gadgets float through and activate this fragmentation of rational form. The car and airplane, which render our everyday understanding of ordered space absurd, reach their logical conclusion. In fact, these tools now provide order and coherence to an architecture that is only a simulatory framed representation of abstraction and logic.[5]

Hodgetts and his partner, Ming Fung proposed another, grimmer prospect for the 1988 film *Nightfall*. The incomplete forms of Arcosanti, an architectural commune located in the high desert

HODGETTS & FUNG
DESIGN ASSOCIATES
Ecotopia Film Project
1981

of Arizona, provided the setting. Arcosanti remains the most viable attempt to actually build another world. Founded by the Italian architect Paolo Soleri in 1970, the commune experiments with what its leader calls "arcology...a methodology that recognizes the necessity for radical reorganization of the sprawling urban landscape into densely integrated, three-dimensional towns and cities."[6] One city resembles crystalline formations that have coalesced around a core of surfaces – Buckminster Fuller's Dymaxion House expanded into an organic urban center. Another city of large earthforms alters the landscape on the outside while completely controlling the environment within. Floating collections of cells spread over a sea of either land or water. Soleri's cities combine a Baudrillardian vision of the cellular nature of space in technological society with a romantic, Corbusian vision of a planet in which ninety percent of the ground has been freed by the concentration of human activity. Ironically, the result is that the interiorized beehives of rationality proclaimed by science fiction films are reproduced.[7]

As in all utopian dreams, these megalomaniacal visions represent a society based on the communal

PAOLO SOLERI
foundry apse
Arcosanti
Arcosanti, Arizona, 1977
Photo: Ivan Pintar

PAOLO SOLERI
critical mass model
Arcosanti
Arcosanti, Arizona, 1970
Photo: Tomiaki Tamura

recrafting of the world so that it becomes more diversified, responsive, and technologically enabling. The fragmentary nature of the first of Soleri's cities to go under construction unintentionally asserts this dream. The three percent of Arcosanti currently completed represents a curious mixture of forms. A concrete frame restaurant and administration building looks like an unfinished piece of brutalist architecture. Another administration building has all the anonymous charm of a 1970s social services

PAOLO SOLERI
visitors center
Arcosanti
Arcosanti, Arizona, 1974
Photo: Aaron Betsky

center designed by followers of Charles Moore. The community's formative grand arch resembles both the apse in Hadrian's Villa and a bandshell. Compelling unfinished shapes promise perfection in their casual gesture towards it. Concrete beams extend into space, suggesting further grids; tension members are elaborate, carved, and colored, as if to coax out the power of their hidden forces. The whole complex resembles the nearby ruins of the Anasazi Indians. A small arcadian plot of land in the valley below the community gives this nostalgic commune an agricultural basis.

Arcosanti's mythic rather than futuristic qualities ultimately create its charm. They propose a society whose recognizable forms and romantic clinging to the earth evoke either the ruins of a former civilization, the foundation of a future civilization, or simply the architecture of a group of individuals engaging in craft. In fact, the community supports itself through craft, and by thinking about craft. Context and history have become abstracted, their only function here to construct an alternative world as a day-to-day activity. However, Arcosanti depends on the sale of its products, and this atmosphere of production violates the organic self-building of the community. While Paolo Soleri continues to dream of ever more refined technological wonders, such as a Pulse Bridge adjusting itself to the weight passing over its surface, and new arcologies projected into space, Arcosanti remains a place where architects can engage in the mythic activity of building another world as an integral part of the activities of daily life.

PAOLO SOLERI
section
Pulse Bridge Project
New York, New York, 1988
Photo: Tomiaki Tamura

At present, the work of **Lebbeus Woods** undoubtedly represents the most compelling mythmaking. Working as an illustrator, he perfects the real-life visions of other architects. Except in the delicacy of his renderings, perfection is difficult to find. Woods's vision is terrifying, and marks the appropriation of cinema's visionary power by architecture. After proposing several perfect observatory spheres and spaceships, he envisioned worlds such as Centricity, a community established after an unnamed holocaust. Centricity's task is to rebuild this world. Its function is architecture, its methodologies those of science. Woods is somewhat idealistic and mystical in his words: "the interplay of metrical systems establishing boundaries of material and energetic forms is the foundation of a universal science (universcience) whose workers include all individuals...."[8] But his drawings are more precise, harrowing, and evocative. What might be termed buildings resemble refineries; there are no office buildings or houses, only the perfection of a laboring science. What appear to be walls mimicking natural cliffs are linear accelerators. Deep inside the vaults of these technological tools, blown up to a monumental

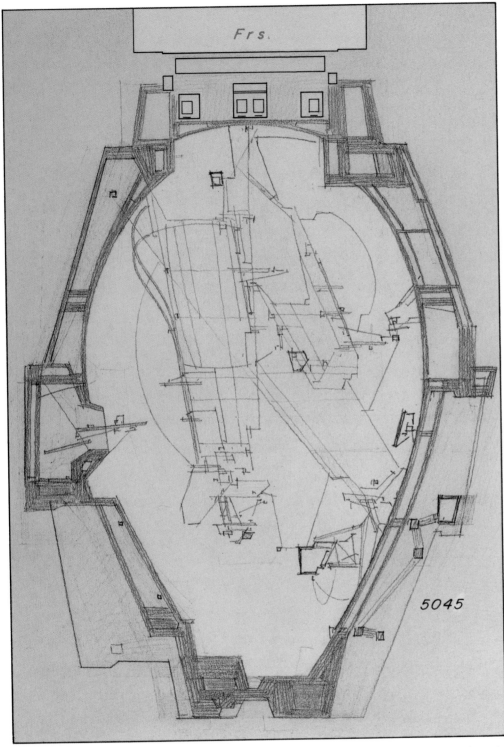

Frs.

5045

LEBBEUS WOODS
Cross Section,
Sector 5045, Quadrant 1
Underground Berlin Project
Berlin, Germany, 1988

scale, lie vast open spaces, articulated only by focal points for the architecture: a chair, a suspended parody of the chaise longue, from which to observe. This is a world of architecture, not the architecture of building and science, but their merger into an evolving, spiraling, and filmic vision recrafting a self-destructive society.

Woods's more recent projects construct worlds that more directly critique current society. He literally cuts away at the skin of the earth and its human encrustations, hollowing out a sphere for architecture below, which he equates with experimental living:

This becomes the site for experimental living, relying on a combination of high technology – for links to other centers across the world – and on very tactile activities, in short the making of things which are instrumental, literally, in experimental living: tools for extending perception at every scale of experience. Living experimentally means life learning about itself.[9]

Here is the purest refinement of the modernist dream, life as nothing more than self-reflection through the medium of technology, technology as the social bond. Architecture is the revelation, realization, and activity of this world, rather than its representation. What Woods proposes is a scientific inversion of the Tower of Babel.[10]

Underground City, a proposed project below the surface of Berlin, is the first realization (at least in drawn form) of this world. Berlin prior to 1989 is seen as the ultimate modern metropolis, victimized first by the

LEBBEUS WOODS
Cross Section
of Vertical Settlement
Terra Nova Project
1989

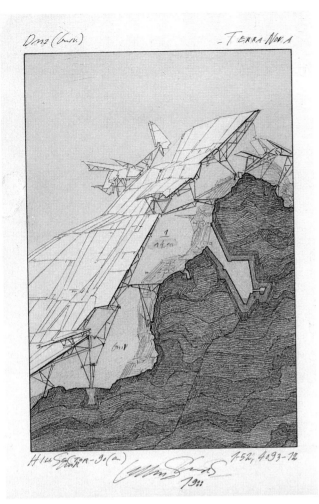

irrational ends of megalomaniacal rationality, and then by the divisive polarization and urban blight, the drawn-out coda to that victory of modernization. Woods' alternative city builds down, not up, in "inverted towers." "Chamberwalls" mark the limits of the city. The interior of these womb-like walls extends deep into the surface of the earth. This city, according to Woods, denies the contradictions of Berlin and resumes primal contact with the rhythms of the earth. Its architectural elements "vibrate and shift in diverse frequencies, in resonance with the earth and also with one another." Metal plates form a civic network of connected spaces, marking the social connections of the city rather than stages for the appropriation of meaning. Throughout the whole city, in a series of "living laboratories," people only live in the present. Architecture now exists as instruments that "connect the inhabitant with events in the world around him and within himself." Furniture, walls, and machinery are indistinguishable; they all work together as relational tools that extend the self into a community shaped according to natural forces.[11]

Assembled with leftover forms scavenged from above, this kinetic universe creates an archaeology of both the earth and the city. Fragmentary, deformed, and extensive elements trace an unseen geometry or vibration. As the city above decays, Woods postulates, this new way of living will build itself out of the ground, first appearing like a giant, clawing, metallic worm, and then as a leaning tower which both destroys and reconstructs Berlin. Architecture becomes pure projection, and, as construction, will infect the earth and the city, building another world. Because this violent process replaces the myriad contradictions of our society with a perfected society, it is also utopian. Subsequent projects trace the infiltration of this projective architecture to Paris. Without doubt Woods still has the whole world to rebuild.

"I am not a storyteller, I am an architect," Woods states, thus presenting his work as the only possibility for architecture.[12] Clearly a critical modernization can be carried out in and through architecture, dissolving the stable ground of society and selfhood to construct relationships of investigative and experimental craft. Currently, that vision can only exist on paper, in words, and in everything that violates its essential constructive nature while bringing its projective force to ever greater forms of perfection.

1. For a review of utopian and dystopian visions of the twentieth century, see: Corn, Joseph J. (Ed.). *Imagining Tomorrow. History, Technology, and the American Future.* Cambridge, MA: The MIT Press, 1986.

2. *Future Systems.* London: The Architectural Association, 1987.

3. More, Sir Thomas, Saint. *Utopia.* New York: Da Capo Press, 1969 (1516 [Latin], 1551 [English]).

4. *A Style for the Year 2001.* Tokyo: Shinkenchiku Co., Ltd., 1985.

5. Callenbach, Ernest. *Ecotopia.* Berkeley, CA: University of California Press, 1970.

6. Paolo Soleri, quoted in Blumenthal, Ralph. "Futuristic Vision in the Desert." *The New York Times,* February 1, 1987.

7. Soleri, Paolo. *The City in the Image of Man.* Cambridge: MA: The MIT Press, 1969.

8. Woods, Lebbeus. *Centricity. The Unified Urban Field.* Berlin: Aedes Gallery, 1987, p. 12.

9. Woods, Lebbeus. *Onefivefour,* New York: Princeton Architectural Press, 1989.

10. Ibid, p. 8.

11. Ibid, pp. 9-12.

12. Woods, Lebbeus. "Work." Lecture at the Southern California Institute of Architecture, Santa Monica, California, November 30, 1989.

SHIN TAKAMATSU
Nishida Dentist's Office
Kyoto, Japan, 1983

TECHNOMORPHISM

The question of technology lies at the heart of all investigations of how to make an architecture that continues the project of the modern, whether through representation, mapping and mirroring, critical investigation, appropriation and extrapolation, or subversion. If the nature of human intervention in the world is essentially operative, laying down the foundation of human society, then the mechanisms of this extension – first tools and then machines – define our social relations. The complexity of these relationships has reached such a high level that it has become internalized, and any sense of outer coherence is now abstract or invisible. A false sense of the human body and of the limits of the world is established to distinguish between these two, long since destroyed by technology and its consciousness, science. Some philosophers, scientists, and social theoreticians argue that these distinctions are meaningless to begin with. Regardless of the cause – in the intrinsic nature of existence, which we have never clearly understood, in language and all its derivatives, or in the division between labor and ownership – technology's rapid breakdown of the barriers between the body and the world is visible everywhere. Television and travel collapse space and time; heart implants and hormones alter the body; technological artifacts as diverse as eyeglasses and plate glass windows provide variable means of experiencing the world. For many centuries, architecture has stood between humanity and the world. According to persuasive and nostalgic classicists desiring its continuation,[1] architecture represents both, forming a literal and conceptual mediation. But this role has been thoroughly undermined by all aspects of modernization, whether by the trivialization of the profession, the superseding of the logic of three dimensions, the invisibility of new forms of mediation and contact, or the realization that the project of the modern demands destroying any distinction between the body – and thus the object – and the world. Pure technology remains: the act of extension, manipulation and mediation, representation and mapping, which we call self, but which is no longer housed in our bodies. Any architecture of such an extension, a critical action in the world, can only express the same; insofar that it has any shape, that shape must be technomorphic.

Many young architects – *the technomorphists* – are fascinated with a strange hybrid of "building/body/machines." The construction and projection of such technomorphic tools stand in for, consume, and deny both the body and the world, welding them into an operable machine. Much of this fascination is based on the development of machinery which, given all its attributable physical resources, produces much more convincing expressions of modernization than architecture. A stealth bomber has more potency than a shopping mall, and even the complex articulations of a piece of "dead tech" have more vitality than a floor plan. A question arises: how can one work through this fascination and make architecture, fully realizing that the accomplishment of this task is a hopelessly, and therefore hope-filled, romantic one?

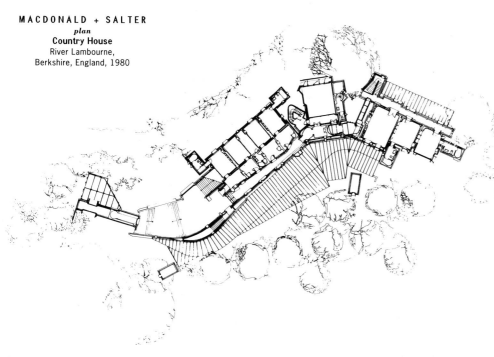

MACDONALD + SALTER
elevation,
bar/service structures
ICI Trade Pavilion,
Royal Agricultural Showground
Stoneleigh, England, 1983

Christopher MacDonald and Peter Salter respond to this problem by taking the merger of biomorphic and high tech forms that the Architectural Association developed in the 1960's one step further. They create shaggy beasts, simple objects with multiple layers of skin deformed in two ways. First, they are made of metal, crafted with a shipbuilder's sense of tectonics. Second, MacDonald and Salter also regard their beasts as natural inhabitants of the landscape that respond to the weather's vagaries and the geographic particulars of their context. They see themselves as alchemists, latter-day blacksmiths engaged in a sacred and romantic task: to forge nature into a tool or mechanism that will metamorphose into a path, boundary, edge, threshold and, eventually, space.[2] The snaky form of the country house in Berkshire, 1986, and the splayed wings of the Oriental Studies Museum Extension at the University of Durham, 1982-83, articulate the site's condition in physical form. One wing of the museum grows out of the ground as a stretched arc. The whole wedge-shaped extension is covered with shaggy plates, balconies, bridges, and seemingly random windows. This strategy is taken further in the ICI Trade Pavilion, 1983, initially formed by columns mimicking both trees and technological risers, and supporting a fan-shaped roof that mediates sunshine. The skin of the building is then "woven" on, leaving little

MACDONALD + SALTER
plan
Country House
River Lambourne,
Berkshire, England, 1980

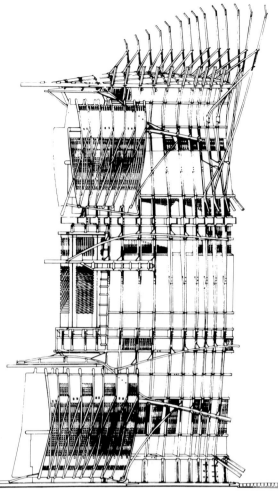

clumps of functional elements protected by its metallic stretch. The architecture is composed of an indefinable network of supports and connections and a series of coverings. The result is very similar to a living being whose skin is packed with organisms connected by nerves and a skeleton, but it is also a machine that converts the landscape into such an organism. The fact that MacDonald and Salter have designed only in the landscape, and that they believe technology can still stand in for the human body while making a stable structure,[3] reveals their underlying romanticism.

Toyo Ito is less interested in the use of stable structures, or even solid forms, than with technology's progressive ephemerality, diminished into invisibility by a complete electronic, and perhaps chemical, abolition of its working parts. Ito expresses the traces, shadows, and scrims that echo this disappearance, and with it our concept of the human being. His building designs use metal, either stretched into scrims, screens, and taut ribs, or used to create minimal surfaces for walls or tables that almost vanish in scale. Ito approaches the urban dweller as a nomad, an ethereal part of the complex urban environment plugging into that envi-

MACDONALD + SALTER
partial elevation
ICI Trade Pavilion,
Royal Agricultural Showground
Stoneleigh, England, 1983

TOYO ITO
Silver Hut
Tokyo, Japan, 1984
Photo: Tomio Ohashi

SHIN TAKAMATSU
Maruto Building IV
(The Orphe Building)
Kyoto, Japan, 1987

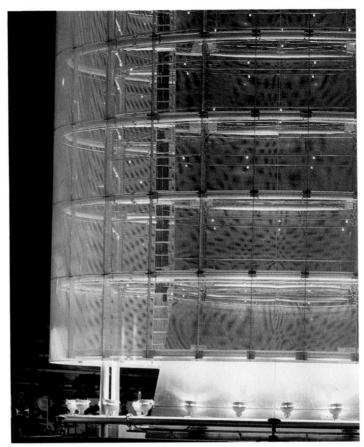

TOYO ITO
The Tower of the Winds
Yokohama City, Japan, 1986
Photo: Shinkenchiku

ronment wherever he or she can give to or gain from it. He designed a nomad house for himself in 1984, a Woman's Nomad House in 1985, and a Nomad Club in 1986. The forms erected around his nomadic creature form the halo of a permanent body created by the temporary connection. His architecture dedicates itself to expressing this void: "What I wish to attain in my architecture is not another nostalgic object, but rather a certain superficiality of expression in order to reveal the nature of the void hidden beneath." In this way, architecture avoids becoming "noth-

ing more than another of the countless consumer codes of the city" – only the equivalent of a display board or monitor remains.[4] This form of *ephemeral technomorphism* is most evident in the 1986 project for the Tower of the Winds, in which a 60-foot high exhaust tower is reclad with perforated aluminum panels positioned in front of an acrylic mirror plate. In between these two confusing skins,

which outline form while refusing materiality, a myriad of lighting effects, created by technology gone wild, reflect the time of day, the passing of the hour, the city rhythm, and the movement of winds. Rather than celebrating man's place in the world, as did the original Tower of the Winds in Athens, this tower celebrates the disappearance of both man and the world in the scrim of technology.[5]

Ito's compatriot, Shin Takamatsu, also celebrates this disappearance but with considerably more exuberance and violence. His buildings are frightening reminders of a declining industrial world. He takes our industrial wasteland, polishes it up, streamlines it, and puts it on display. The Nishida Dentist's Office, 1983, resembles a giant turbine marooned in the city. Its windows are narrow slits between battle-strength drainpipes. Placed below bolted metal turrets, they march meaninglessly down the facade like their neo-Gothic counterparts. The only face the building presents to the world is a porthole bolted onto the concrete at the narrow end. This architecture does not express structure or function, scale or context. It only wishes to be a machine treated respectfully. The details, metal plates, windows, and tubes – screwed onto an otherwise anonymous concrete box – are its architecture. The interiors of Takamatsu's buildings are fragmented or empty. In the Pharaoh Building, 1986, structure becomes an overabundance of white-painted vertical and horizontal planes, some pulled apart to admit

SHIN TAKAMATSU
Asano Dentist's Office
Kyoto, Japan, 1984

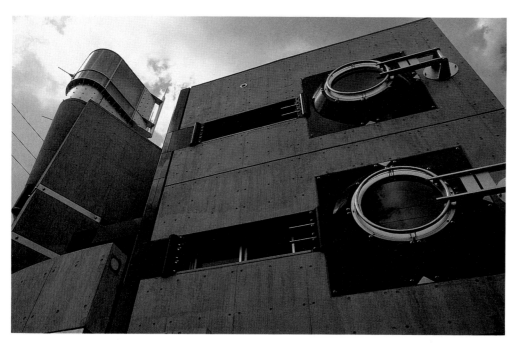

light, others supporting a piece of what appears to be an orthogonal concrete frame. The Maruto Building IV, 1987, presents itself to the world as a set of watchtowers, replete with gunslots lashed together with metal rods that cut into the concrete skin of the building. This is heavy metal building. Takamatsu represents the enigmatic, ominous side of technomorphism. These buildings may be mythic fragments of a lost civilization, a dead tech, or perhaps the prototypes for battleships that conquer space, or they may merely be exaggerated and animated fragments of our surrounding technological world that we tend to ignore in daily life. In each instance, they destroy all traditional accoutrements of architecture, thumbing their noses at humanistic understanding. A new force is loose in the world; and this is its already outdated, or perhaps purposefully and frighteningly recognizable, mask.[6]

MORPHOSIS
ARCHITECTS
plan
2-4-6-8 House
Venice, California, 1978

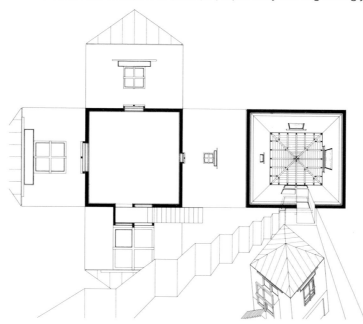

The Los Angeles firm of **Morphosis** shares a profound interest in dead tech, also wishing to build the more terrifying aspects of our society – the violence that is intrinsic to human society and that has a technological character. Thom Mayne and Michael Rotondi, the partners, believe that to articulate this violence begins a descriptive act. Their buildings are representational systems that describe the act of the construction and the act of representation itself. This self-reflexive form of technomorphism seeks to dissolve the making of buildings into the act of architecture as it articulates technology.

Early works, such as the 2-4-6 House, 1980, were concerned with geometry and the language of architecture. Morphosis subsequently used architecture as a *"feedback loop"* whose obsessive reiteration of the formal result of layering one syntax (compositional form) back onto the original composition created a dense commentary. This description of the inherent complexity and internal contradictions, which architecture's need for consistency demands, is also found in their densely layered drawings. The Crawford House, 1990, overlays the contradictory geometries of the global Mercator grid with an experiential axis and a functional axis in order to release open spaces that become the reality of the house. Through a slippage in the tectonics of architecture, both the Crawford House and the Comprehensive Cancer Clinic reveal the beautiful inadequacy of their systems: broken grids and walls so flat that they become objects. These incompletions allow use and indicate the possibility for continual change. This humanism is further developed in buildings that articulate natural forces. In 72 Market Street Restaurant, 1981, a central column acts as an earthquake ten-

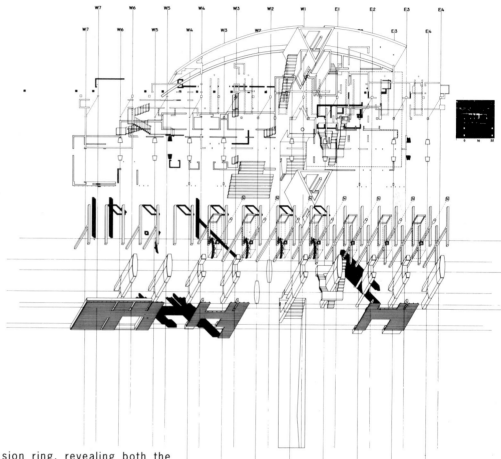

sion ring, revealing both the potential for destruction and man's ability to alter its inevitability. In the Venice III House, 1983, weights and pulleys control "sun-sails" that respond to the wind and sun, changing the physical aspect of the house from an unfinished ruin to a temporary tent. The impulse is to make an architecture describing the possibility for human action, rather than a static representation of a mediator

MORPHOSIS
ARCHITECTS
interior
72 Market Street Restaurant
Venice, California, 1983

between man and the world. Architecture becomes an operable mediator. The enclosure of interior space and the fulfillment of axes are less important than this gadget-like breakdown of an imposed system into a collection of usable tools.

Morphosis both updates modernism's formality, making it more responsive to current needs, and continues its didacticism in a more veiled manner. The Sixth Street House, 1987, strips away the stucco covering on a standard suburban house, revealing the lath below. The upper story is composed of a grandly symmetrical facade, which makes order out of the act of uncovering. The interior of the *piano nobile* above the lower apartment is one large room without any functional parameters, invaded by giant pieces of technology. For Thom Mayne, they represent the reality of the industrial world whose existence lies beyond the fragmentary orders of the immediate context to which the facade responds. These gesturing hunks of steel have internalized modernization's *sturm und drang*. The objects become the actual mechanism by which one lives in the space: windows, doors, bathrooms, and HVAC units. Architecture here is not about space,

**MORPHOSIS
ARCHITECTS**
exterior
Venice III House
Venice, California, 1982
Photo: Aaron Betsky

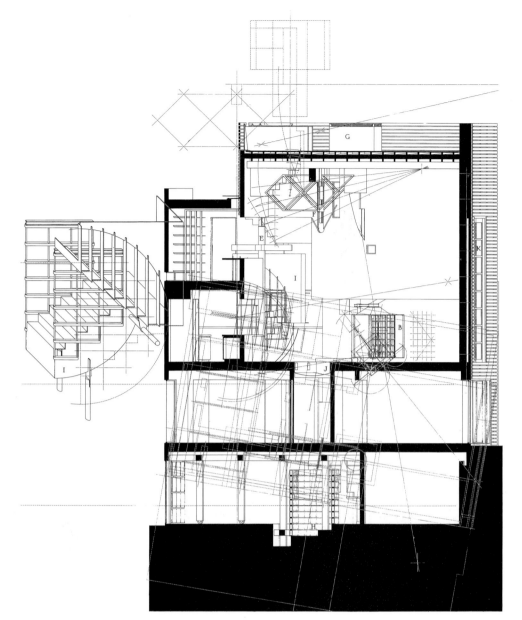

function, or scale, but about the creation of a set of mechanistic relations, condensing the outside world to a level that it can be worked on, and extending the body to a scale and efficacy capable of working on that world.[7]

Trained by Morphosis, **Michele Saee** takes his forms to rhetorical heights. Working with the same vocabulary of steel plates, kinetic members, cantilevered lights, and posed plywood panels, Saee makes everything a little bigger. His architectural fragments become heavy to the touch and grander in scale – a more *Piranesian technomorphism* that also makes more direct connections to both the outside world and the body. Saee sees his buildings as a new kind of billboard, but not one that sells. Angeli Trattoria, 1988, is a dark and blank facade, a sign of absence. The Ecru Store, 1988, is made up of welded steel plates that vaguely spell out the name of the store. One enters through these sinuous plates, and finds

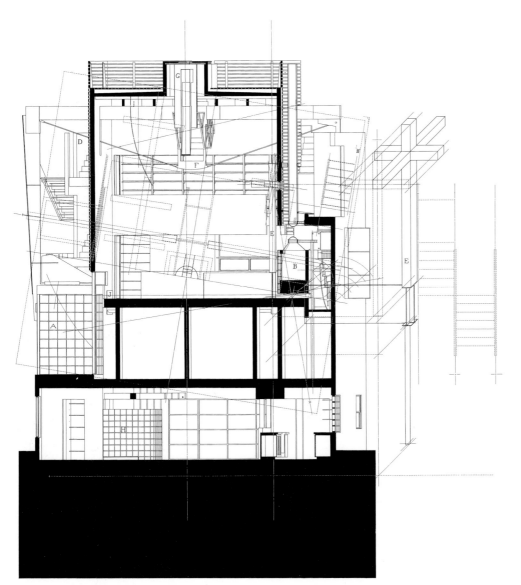

MICHELE SAEE
architectural drawing/collage
1989

two sets of rectangles whose walls have been cut to let in light, leaving windows bowed under the impact, and connected by an insect-like display piece looming over a narrow passage. The interior world of Saee's projects is an overwhelming collection of crafted fragments of perverse functionality, the exterior an enigmatic pose. According to Saee, through craft, these poses, which are based on the human body, have been collaged and blown up to the scale of a public sign. Gleefully accepting the extensive urban field of Los Angeles' anti-humanistic tendencies, the welding, composing, and construction of his architecture erase distinctions, creating new connections that stand in for what it has destroyed. Architecture is reduced to a pure sign, a facade or face that has been decomposed into nothing but sinews, tendons, and other mechanistic versions of our own innards. What is missing is that order "in between," the overall coherence traditionally allowing us to recognize another human being or a building.

MICHELE SAEE
exterior
Angeli Trattoria Restaurant
Los Angeles, California, 1988
Photo: Peter Cook

194

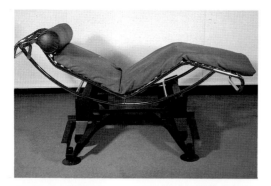

**HOLT, HINSHAW,
PFAU, JONES**
Chaise Longue
1988

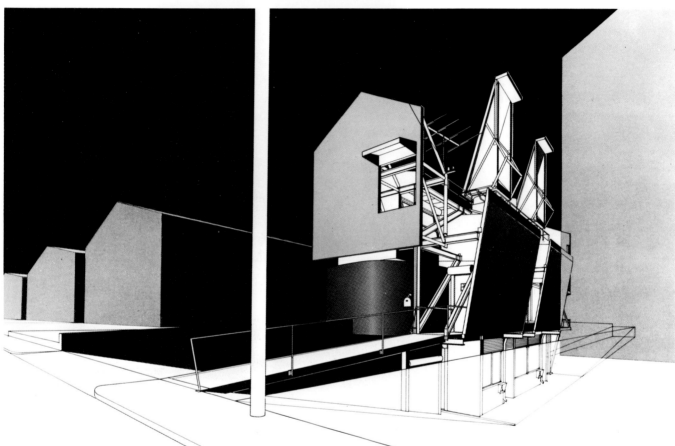

**HOLT, HINSHAW,
PFAU, JONES**
plan (above) and perspective
Tract House Project
Manhattan Beach, California,
1986

The technomorphism of Wes Jones and Peter Pfau, of the San Francisco firm Holt, Hinshaw, Pfau, Jones, is even more aggressively romantic. Their small fable, written in 1987, posits an alternative to modernism's reductivist and abstracting urge. Why did architecture disappear as an expressive medium, they ask, responding, "We postulate: alien intervention." They claim that during the summer of 1917, Le Corbusier was visited by aliens who were frightened by the successes of modernization. Realizing that architecture, according to Pfau and Jones, was the means for "establishing" this process, the aliens steered Le Corbusier towards self-destruction in the endless pursuit of his own disappearance. In opposition to such an urge, Pfau and Jones argue for an expressive architecture – not one directly representational, since technology is becoming increasingly abstract and invisible,[8] *but an architecture that is an object of excess.* Appropriating the images of production – factories, backhoes, and refineries – their architecture blows these icons up to the point that they become giant "gobots," Japanese toys that can be transformed from human beings to machines to buildings with a facility architects can only dream of. This architecture simultaneously parodies consumable items. They claim that through the neutrality achieved by this contradiction, their architecture is now free to create a flexible, usable mechanism for reclaiming the world.[9]

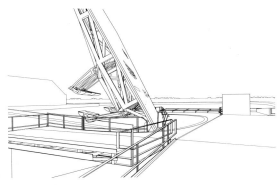

Some of their projects are just machines, suggesting that we reestablish the perceived world as an area to be worked on, rather than as a stable field. Pfau and Jones designed a primitive hut that unfolds, gathers, moves, and changes its appearance as the paradigmatic commencement of a new architecture. The 1984 Tract House converts a narrow suburban lot into the ultimate suburban machine, churning up grids and trash into an explosion of metallic connections.[10] The vocabulary is one of steel plates, fragmented grids, and, especially, erector-set-like connections based on the construction of things that make buildings possible: cranes, diggers, and scaffolding. Architecture disappears into its own construction, and becomes a heroic, romantically ideal object. The 1988 project for the Astronauts Memorial becomes an armature holding up a metal mirror to the sky. The armature tracks the sun so that the mirror always reflects the light. The names of astronauts who died are inscribed on its surface. People and nature have become only language and reflections, a mirage on an invisible surface tracked by the only physical reality, a kinetic piece of heroic construction. Holt, Hinshaw, Pfau, Jones presents a new kind of monumentality. Absent are those orders supposedly controlling what is remembered by providing a cultural context. Instead, only a mirror, a complicated set of pistons, and metal members keep the piece constantly in motion. Architecture, in the sense that all architecture is a monument, once again disappears, leaving behind a new kind of romantic expressionism, a building that fades into the image of a new nature – that of technology rather than a man-made vision of nature.

**HOLT, HINSHAW,
PFAU, JONES**
perspectives
**Astronauts Memorial,
Kennedy Space Center**
Cape Canaveral, Florida, 1988

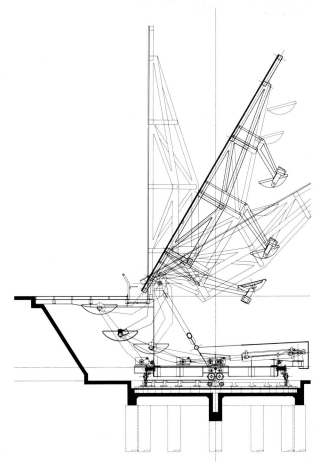

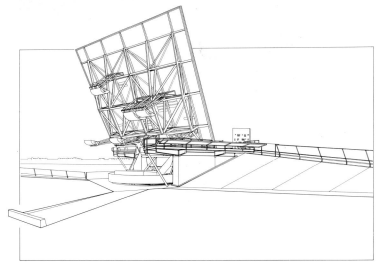

**HOLT, HINSHAW,
PFAU, JONES**
section
**Astronauts Memorial,
Kennedy Space Center**
Cape Canaveral, Florida, 1988

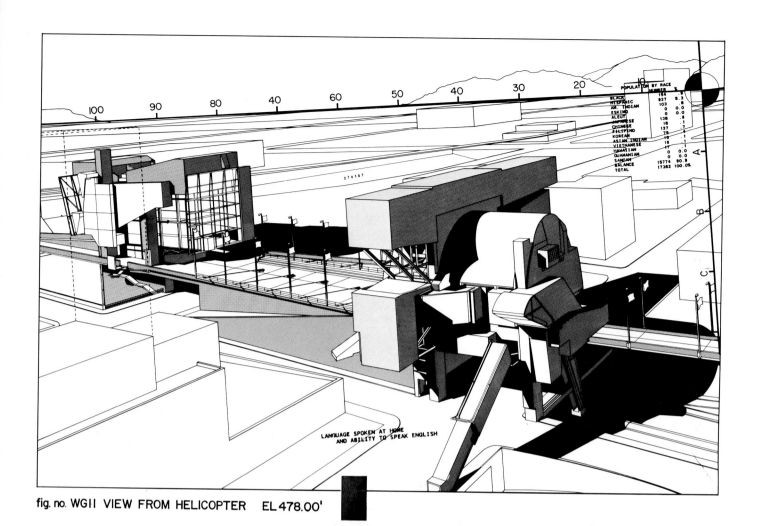

fig. no. WGII VIEW FROM HELICOPTER   EL 478.00'

NEIL DENARI
perspective
**West Coast Gateway
Competition Project**
Los Angeles, California, 1988

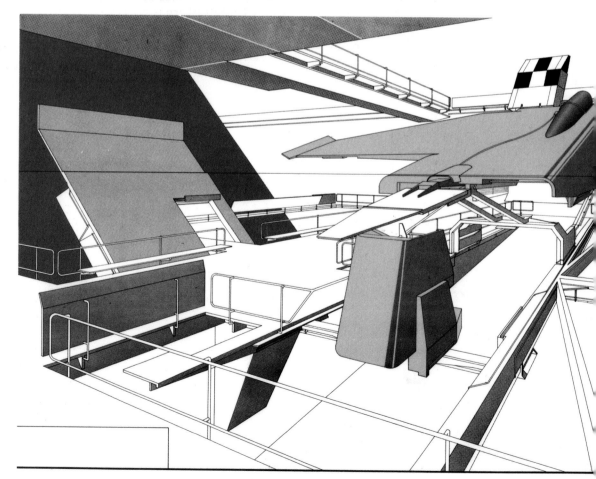

NEIL DENARI
perspective
**God Part Zero,
Tokyo Forum Competition
Project**
Tokyo, Japan, 1989

NEIL DENARI
model
**God Part Zero,
Tokyo Forum Competition
Project**
Tokyo, Japan, 1989

Neil Denari has a love for the mechanistic side of architecture, but he is more involved with the representation of the instability of science than in the expressive potential of the architectural object. His forms are based on helicopters, airplanes, and boats – machines that float through the air and on the sea, and whose forms are indistinguishable from their function and context, yet have an enigmatic scale. These useful "beasts" extend our bodies into space, while imprisoning and subjecting us to their will. By recasting these objects, Denari exorcises them, exerting a complete control over their construction and use. He obsessively reiterates the bullnosed form as his central organizing space, suspending it from overscaled grids. His project for the Tower of London, 1986, is a giant bullnosed clock riding on rails over the top of the prison, marking both its boundaries and time. The clock locates and articulates both the direct context and the larger cosmological coordinates. It is a "noematachograph" that retains its illusive and enigmatic presence.[11] Denari's projects remain closed and enigmatic containers vibrating with the power of a hidden technology. The West Coast-Gateway Competition, 1988, proposes a hulking presence floating over the freeway. Made out of metal plates, it is a blank reflector of activities, forever refusing to pose as a finished form or ordering device. Its ends are cut off; it is groundless, and also lacks scaling devices, except for the structure's musculature bulging out from underneath the metallic armature.[12] Lately, Denari's bullnosed forms have begun to resemble whales. An Ahab searching for the great white whale of architecture, Denari acknowledges danger, obsession, and sheer loud noise as a necessary substitute for the soothing platitudes of culture. Architecture, like science, is an ultimately self-destructive search for the self.[13]

A more prosaic version of this kind of technomorphism is created by the **Interim Office of Architecture** in San Francisco. Working in former Army barracks now housing the Headlands Center for the Arts in Marin County, these young architects replaced straight pipes with flextube, made an insect-like towel and condom dispenser, and used steel doors to segregate the various sectors of privacy in this raw space. The mirror of the machine glorifies the most prosaic functions

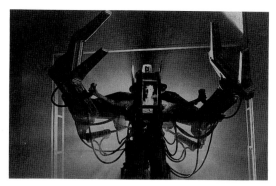

of the body, and the machine takes on a biomorphic quality.

The architecture resembles suits worn in such science fiction films as *Aliens*. A person disappears into the robot, sees reality through a monitor mounted in a helmet, and works in space through mechanistic expansions of his or her own body. The suit is both a space station, a condensed version of that most refined piece of architecture, and a mask of the self.

INTERIM OFFICE OF ARCHITECTURE
Granite Cooktop
1985

Some students take technomorphic architecture and the logical consequences of its development very seriously. **Steven Flusty**, designing an arts center in 1989 at the Southern California Institute of Architecture in Los Angeles, created a stack of containers for making and producing art, a parking garage for its viewing and performance, a control tower for its advertisement and internal facilitation, and a machine for living – a giant swimming pool placed on top of minimal (and space-capsule-like) living cells. His architecture of fragments borrows from disciplines such as engineering, shipping, space, and advertising, and responds to specific tasks without falling back on a false coherence.

STEVEN FLUSTY
model
Arts Center Project for Culver City
Southern California Institute of Architecture Studio
Santa Monica, California, 1989

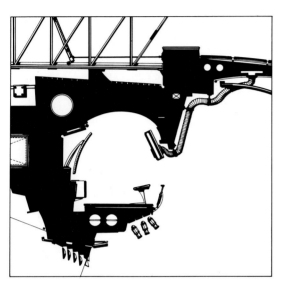

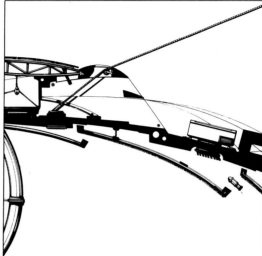

EDWARD WEBB
section details
Opera House Project
University of California
at Los Angeles Studio
Los Angeles, California, 1988

The 1988 design for an opera house by U.C.L.A. student Edward Webb did not even present an object. Robot-like machines that performed various pieces of the architectural program were meticulously drawn and diagrammatically explained. In one fleeting moment, the whole complex appeared in a set of slides revealing the designer operating the pieces underneath the architectural armature. The possibility that architecture could ever achieve this level of fragmentation or performance remains doubtful, but the goal has been stated by other students, and remains a task to be worked on.

Technomorphists realize that architecture is a self-conscious technology. Although a hybrid between man and machine has fascinated artists since the myth of Icarus, these latest monsters are not, as were Picabia's and Duchamp's, industrial substitutes for sexual reproduction that allow man to procreate without humanity. Nor are they merely functional tools, which would be the final victory of the engineer and the self-expressive logic of a system eternally seeking control and domination through its own invisibility. Technomorphic architecture replaces the self with suits of armor preventing its destruction – elaborate gadgets shedding all pretensions of that useless protruberance on the face of the city, architecture, and its final haven (or prison). It neither promises a new Jerusalem nor a Piranesian prison, but instead sets out to work. Its advocates believe that the body can extend itself into space and engage the world – an extension that requires a technological transformation of the self. The conceit of technomorphism is that such a transformation also, somewhat miraculously, preserves that illusive quality, humanity.

Writing from the landscape of Los Angeles, one must believe in such a possibility. Lost in the endless grids that stretch out their artificial unintelligibility over an abstract landscape, we survive only by way of the mediation of space through cars, of air through HVAC systems, and human contact through electronic devices. The contradictory orders of houses, office buildings, and cultural landmarks have become confusing elements in a

landscape often negotiated with fear and loathing, and with faith only in the machine. "We should stop trying to design better buildings and start learning how to design better cars," says architect Craig Hodgetts. Yet automobiles are only compacted technology hidden by consumer styling, and may even eventually become unnecessary. We need an architecture that both explains and justifies itself as the realization of the process of modernization, not as the temporary occurrences of stable form dropped off in that process. We need an architecture that refuses to limit itself to two choices – to resist modernization or to make a Faustian bargain with its reality. Architects must realize that the processes of daily life are also the processes of modernization. Socialization, sense-making, and consciousness compose our visual field. Craft must create a means of providing empowerment. Consequently, the only honest approach acknowledges that perfection is both a technological task and an unattainable ideal. Every architectural act is a constructive violation.

1. Alexander Tzoniz and Liane Lefaivre provide one of the latest and most thoughtful examples: *Classical Architecture. The Poetics of Order*. Cambridge, MA: The MIT Press, 1986.

2. Conversation with Peter Salter, April 24, 1989, London.

3. MacDonald, Christopher, and Peter Salter. *Building Projects MacDonald+Salter*. New York: Storefront for Art and Architecture, 1987.

4. Ito, Toyo."Collage and Superficiality in Architecture." Frampton, Kenneth. *A New Wave of Japanese Architecture*. New York: The Institute for Architecture and Urban Studies, 1978, p. 68.

5. Ito, Toyo. "The Tower of Winds." *Japan Architect*, May, 1987, pp. 12-14.

6. "Shin Takamatsu." *SD*, January 1988, pp. 7-204.

7. Mayne, Thom, and Michael Rotondi. *Morphosis. Buildings and Projects*. New York: Rizzoli International Publications, 1990.

8. Jones, Wes, and Peter Pfau. Unpublished manuscript, 1987.

9. Jones, Wes. Lecture at the Southern California Institute for Architecture, March 22, 1989, Santa Monica, California; conversation with author, April 3, 1989, Los Angeles, California.

10. Pfau, Peter, and Wes Jones. "Pfau/Jones - Holt & Hinshaw." McCarter, Robert (Ed.) *Building Machines*. New York: Princeton Architectural Press, 1987, pp. 42-60.

11. *The London Project*. New York: Princeton Architectural Press, 1989, Chapter 3.

12. Denari, Neil. "Neil Denari." *Building Machines*, pp. 14-27.

13. Conversations with author, Los Angeles, January, 1989.

INDEX

*italicized numbers
indicate illustrations*